FORESIGHT

FORESIGHT

HOW THE CHEMISTRY OF LIFE REVEALS PLANNING AND PURPOSE

MARCOS EBERLIN

SEATTLE   DISCOVERY INSTITUTE PRESS   2019

Description

Learn about jumping insects with real gears, and the ingenious technology behind a power-punching shrimp. Enter the strange world of carnivorous plants. And check out a microscopic protein machine in a bird's eye that may work as a GPS device by harnessing quantum entanglement. Join renowned Brazilian scientist Marcos Eberlin as he uncovers a myriad of artful solutions to major engineering challenges in chemistry and biology, solutions that point beyond blind evolution to the workings of an attribute unique to minds—foresight.

Library Cataloging Data

Foresight: How the Chemistry of Life Reveals Planning and Purpose by Marcos Eberlin

172 pages, 6 x 9 x 0.37 inches & 0.53 lb, 229 x 152 x 9.3 mm. & 0.240 kg

Library of Congress Control Number: 2019937734

ISBN-13 978-1-936599-65-3 (paperback), 978-1-936599-66-0 (Kindle), 978-1-936599-67-7 (EPUB)

BISAC: SCI007000 SCIENCE / Life Sciences / Biochemistry

BISAC: SCI008000 SCIENCE / Life Sciences / Biology

BISAC: SCI027000 SCIENCE / Life Sciences / Evolution

BISAC: SCI015000 SCIENCE / Cosmology

BISAC: SCI075000 SCIENCE / Philosophy & Social Aspects

Publisher Information

Discovery Institute Press, 208 Columbia Street, Seattle, WA 98104

Internet: http://www.discoveryinstitutepress.com/

Published in the United States of America on acid-free paper.

First Edition, First Printing, May 2019.

Endorsements

I am happy to recommend this to those interested in the chemistry of life. The author is well established in the field of chemistry and presents the current interest in biology in the context of chemistry. I am happy to recommend the work.

—Sir John B. Gurdon, PhD, Nobel Prize in
Physiology or Medicine (2012), Co-Founder of The
Gurdon Institute, University of Cambridge

An interesting study of the part played by foresight in biology.

—Brian David Josephson, PhD, Nobel Prize in Physics (1973),
Professor Emeritus of Physics, University of Cambridge

It's my pleasure to highly recommend the book *Foresight* by Dr. Marcos Eberlin as excellent and instructive material. This book provides masterful information about teleology, an exciting and prominent scientific field that provides irrefutable evidence of foresight in nature. The arguments raised in the book are convincingly supported by incontestable and previously published experimental data, much of it gathered from prestigious scientific journals. Dr. Marcos Eberlin brilliantly makes use of his expertise, achieved in more than twenty-five years applying mass spectrometry in assorted areas such as biochemistry, biology, and fundamental chemistry to outline a convincing case that will captivate even the more skeptical readers. Eberlin's book demonstrates that the currently available scientific knowledge increasingly points to the existence of a supreme being who carefully planned the universe and life. This breakthrough will revolutionize science in the years to come.

—Rodinei Augusti, PhD, Full Professor of Chemistry, Federal
University of Minas Gerais, Belo Horizonte, Brazil

Despite the immense increase of knowledge during the past few centuries, there still exist important aspects of nature for which our scientific understanding reaches its limits. Eberlin describes in a concise manner a large number of such phenomena, ranging from life to astrophysics. Whenever in the past such a limit was reached, faith came into play. Eberlin calls this principle 'foresight.' Regardless of whether one shares Eberlin's approach, it is definitely becoming clear that nature is still full of secrets which are beyond our rational understanding and force us to humility.

—Gerhard Ertl, PhD, Nobel Prize in Chemistry (2007),
Former Director of the Department of Physical Chemistry, Fritz
Haber Institute of the Max Planck Society, Berlin, Germany

Marcos Eberlin, one of the best chemists in the world today, has written a must-read, superb book for anyone considering what indeed science says of the universe and life.

—Dr. Maurício Simões Abrão, Professor at the University of
São Paulo Medical School, São Paulo, Brazil, Editor-in-Chief
of the *Journal of Endometriosis and Pelvic Pain Disorders*

Why would a man stand against an army? Perhaps the man is crazy. Perhaps he wants to commit suicide. Or just maybe the man has some very powerful weapons. Prof. Marcos Eberlin is this man. In *Foresight*, Eberlin challenges an almost universally accepted theory. What are his weapons for attacking such a strong fortress? It is your choice to agree or not with his evidence and arguments. You may in the end conclude he is right, or that he is indeed mad. But to understand Eberlin's side and to be intellectually honest, this is a must-read book.

—Brenno A. D. Neto, PhD, Professor of Chemistry,
University of Brasília, Brasília, Brazil, Associate Editor for
RSC Advances, a journal of the Royal Society of Chemistry

Foresight fascinated me by its breadth and depth of knowledge of all things biological. Drawing from his specific field of chemistry, Marcos Eberlin reveals the astonishing ways that the chemistry of DNA and RNA make them perfect for their tasks. If you ever wondered in biology class why RNA uses ribose and DNA uses deoxyribose, or why RNA uses uracil and DNA thymine, Marcos Eberlin's book will tell you why, and how their perfect suitability for their purpose is a remarkable example of foresight. As Eberlin's detailed description reveals, the chemistry and biology of DNA and RNA come together in an interlocking puzzle that goes click when it's all in place. The fit, and the foresight required to build it, are incredible. Eberlin's book also deals with life on the organismal level—everything from our sense organs to sexual reproduction and the wondrous structure of a bird's egg. None of his foresight arguments are based on a lack of knowledge, or a God-of-the-gaps-mentality. They are based on positive knowledge of what the biochemistry and physiology of life require.

—Ann Gauger, PhD, Senior Fellow, Center for Science
and Culture, Co-Author, *Science and Human Origins*

In his newest book, *Foresight*, award-winning and prominent researcher Prof. Marcos Eberlin cogently responds to crucial questions about life's origin, using an arsenal of current scientific data. Eberlin illustrates his points with varied examples that reveal incredible foresight in planning for biochemical systems. From cellular membranes, the genetic code, and human reproduction, to the chemistry of the atmosphere, birds, sensory organs, and carnivorous plants, the book is a light of scientific good sense amid the darkness of naturalistic ideology.

—Kelson Mota, PhD, Professor of Chemistry,
Amazon Federal University, Manaus, Brazil

Foresight is for those willing to challenge themselves with a new perspective, for free people who dare to go beyond scientific dogmas. Marcos Eberlin's book is a journey through the evidence in chemistry and biology for the indispensable role of foresight in the origin of life and the universe, presented by the author in an easily understood and engaging way.

—Daniela de Luna Martins, PhD, Associate Professor of
Chemistry, Fluminense Federal University, Rio de Janeiro, Brazil

Foresight provides refreshing new evidence, primarily from biology, that science needs to open its perspective on the origin of living things to account for the possibility that purely natural, materialistic evolution cannot account for these facts. The book is written in an easy-to-read style that will be appreciated by scientists and non-scientists alike and encourages the reader to follow the truth wherever it leads, as Socrates advised long ago.

—Michael T. Bowers, PhD, Distinguished Professor, Department of Chemistry and Biochemistry, University of California Santa Barbara

DEDICATION

To my loving wife Elisabeth, my daughters Thais,
Livia and Niina, my son Nicholas,
and my grandchildren Leah, Claire, Theo, Luca and Thomas,
who have followed or, I deeply trust, will follow
the evidence where it leads. And above all, to the "Foresighter."

CONTENTS

ENDORSEMENTS 5

DEDICATION. 9

1. FORESIGHT IN LIFE 13

2. A WORLD FORESEEN FOR BIOCHEMISTRY 25

3. THE CODE OF LIFE 45

4. LIFE'S HELPERS 63

5. BACTERIA, BUGS, AND CARNIVOROUS PLANTS 83

6. BIRDS: A CASE STUDY IN FORESIGHT 99

7. FORESIGHT IN THE HUMAN FORM: REPRODUCTION 109

8. PLANNING FOR THE SENSES 123

9. FORESIGHT AND THE FUTURE OF SCIENCE. 137

ENDNOTES 149

ACKNOWLEDGMENTS 163

ILLUSTRATION CREDITS. 165

INDEX 167

1. Foresight in Life

BIOLOGY IS IN THE MIDST OF A GOLD RUSH OF DISCOVERY. AT MY previous academic institution, the University of Campinas in São Paulo, Brazil, I ran the Thomson Mass Spectrometry Laboratory for twenty-five years. There my team and I delved into many areas of chemistry, biochemistry, and medical science that until recently were still too new to have names—everything from proteomics, lipidomics, and mass spectrometry imaging to petroleomics and bacteria fingerprinting.

My research, along with my role as president of the Brazilian Mass Spectrometry Society and the International Mass Spectrometry Foundation, has brought me into contact with other leading researchers in Brazil and around the globe. And when we come together at conferences, the excitement is palpable. Thanks to a cluster of breakthrough technologies and techniques, almost every week reveals some new wonder in the biological realm.

Some of these discoveries yield new medicines or medical techniques, such as the abundantly awarded cancer pen recently developed by my daughter Livia. Others give engineers new ideas for inventions in the burgeoning field of biomimetics. Still others have no immediate practical application; they're just revelations of beautiful biological ingenuity—scientific discovery for its own sake.

All of this new knowledge is exhilarating in its own right. At the same time I am now convinced that many of these discoveries, taken together, point beyond themselves to something even more extraordinary. This new age of discovery is revealing a myriad of artful solutions to major engineering challenges, solutions that for all the world appear to require something that matter alone lacks. I will put this as plainly as I can: This rush of discovery seems to point beyond any purely blind evolutionary process to the workings of an attribute unique to minds—foresight.

And yes, I know: We're told that it's out of bounds for science to go there. We will take up that claim in subsequent chapters. But regardless of where you ultimately land on the question of what conclusions science should or shouldn't allow, and whether or not you ultimately affirm that this gold rush of new evidence points to the workings of foresight, I urge you to inspect the evidence. Curiosity may have killed the cat, but it's done wonders for the scientific enterprise.

The many and ingenious examples uncovered in recent years are so numerous they could fill many large volumes. The pages that follow highlight only a small fraction of the total. But that fraction is filled with marvels. We'll look at everything from insect gears and power-punching shrimp to carnivorous plants and a protein machine in the avian eye that may harness quantum entanglement, allowing birds to see Earth's magnetic field.

We begin, however, with an example that appears mundane—though only at first glance.

A Membrane and Its Channels

LIFE THRIVES in our diverse planetary environment, thanks in no small part to the many ways Earth is fine-tuned for life. But Earth can also be extremely hostile to life. The oxygen molecule (O_2) is, for instance, essential to life; but only a life form that can efficiently wrap and transport the devil O_2 exactly to a place where it can be used as an energy source would benefit from its angel side. Otherwise, O_2 becomes life's greatest enemy.

Rupture the membrane of a living cell, exposing it to the air, and you will see the great damage O_2 and a myriad of other chemical invaders can do to a perforated cell. Death would be swift and sure. From an engineering standpoint, then, it was essential that a way be found to protect the cell, life's most basic unit. The solution was clever: The cell was surrounded by a strong chemical shield, from the very beginning.

It is often said that a solution always brings with it two additional problems, and a cellular membrane shield is no exception. A simple shield could indeed protect the cell interior from deadly invaders, but such a barrier would also prevent cell nutrients from reaching the inside of the cell, and it would trap cellular waste within. Small neutral molecules could pass through the membrane, but not larger and normally electrically charged biomolecules. A simple shield would be a recipe for swift, sure death. For early cells to survive and reproduce, something more sophisticated was needed. Selective channels through these early cell membranes had to be in place right from the start.

Cells today come with just such doorways, specialized protein channels used in transporting many key biomolecules and ions. How was this selective transport of both neutral molecules and charged ions engineered? Evolutionary theory appeals to a gradual, step-by-step process of small mutations sifted by natural selection, what is colloquially referred to as *survival of the fittest*. But a gradual step-by-step evolutionary process over many generations seems to have no chance of building such wonders, since there apparently can't be many generations of a cell, or even one generation, until these channels are up and running. No channels, no cellular life.

So then, the key question is: How could the first cells acquire proper membranes and co-evolve the protein channels needed to overcome the permeability problem?

Even some committed evolutionists have confessed the great difficulty here. As Sheref Mansy and his colleagues put it in the journal *Nature*, "The strong barrier function of membranes has made it difficult to understand the origin of cellular life."[1]

And that's putting it delicately. Somehow, a double-layer membrane—flexible, stable, and resistant—needed to be engineered, one that would promptly and efficiently protect the cell from the devastating O_2 permeation, remain stable in aqueous acid media, and ably handle fluctuations in temperature and pH (Figure 1.1). To do all these tasks, the

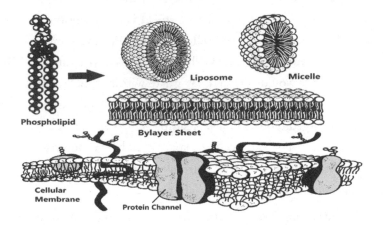

Figure 1.1. The double-layer membrane encloses our cells. It is very flexible, but it also has high mechanical and chemical resistance. The many intricate membrane components and the capacities it possesses that are required to keep a cell alive make the appearance of foresight in the original assembly of the membrane all but overwhelming.

cell's molecular shield also would need a mechanism to sense changes in temperature and pH,[2] and react accordingly, adjusting the membrane's chemical composition to handle these physical and chemical changes.

For instance, as Diego de Mendoza explains, bacterial cells "remodel the fluidity of their membrane bilayer" by incorporating "proportionally more unsaturated fatty acids (or fatty acids with analogous properties) as growth temperature decreases." The process is known as homoviscous adaptation. Cell membranes, in other words, can initiate a series of cellular responses that react to a change in environmental temperature.[3]

If you were to bid this demanding, multifaceted job out to the most technologically advanced engineering firms in the world, their top engineers might either laugh in your face or run screaming into the night. The requisite technology is far beyond our most advanced human know-how. And remember, getting two or three things about this membrane job right—or even 99% of the job—wouldn't be enough. It is all or death! A vulnerable cell waiting for improvements from the gradual Darwinian process would promptly be attacked by a myriad of enemies and die, never to reproduce, giving evolution no time at all to finish the job down the road.

It seems, then, from all the biochemical knowledge we now have, that the cell membrane's many crucial requirements had to be foreseen, and delivered on time, for the earliest cells to survive and reproduce in an aqueous environment.

And that's just the beginning of the foresight apparently required to deliver a membrane good enough to make cellular life viable. Such a membrane wall, with its many intricate abilities, also requires a veritable Swiss Army knife of biomolecules. And happily, these were provided in the form of an amazing class of exquisitely designed biomolecules: the phospholipids (Figure 1.2).

These biomolecular pieces had to be just right. To construct a chemical shield sophisticated enough to allow cells to survive and thrive, there seems to be no substitute for phospholipids. Sometimes I come across articles in journals such as *Science* and *Nature*[4] theorizing about simpler, primordial cell membranes made of "rudimentary" molecules such as fatty acids. But such flights of fancy ignore key chemical details of what's needed to render cellular life viable. Once we confront those details, we

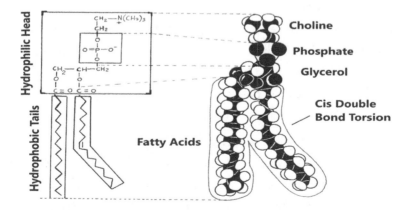

Figure 1.2. This simple caricature only hints at the phospholipids' complex molecular structure.

find that no other biomolecule appears able to sustain life by fulfilling the many intricate roles phospholipids perform.

The structure of a phospholipid can be divided into two main regions that possess quite opposite physical-chemical properties: The head is polar and water-loving (hydrophilic), while the tail is non-polar and water-hating (hydrophobic). This dichotomy of "tastes" is crucial, because it allows for a marvelous trick: In the presence of water, these biomolecules automatically arrange themselves so as to form round, double-layer structures (Figure 1.1) with all the polar heads lining up next to each other and the elongated non-polar tails packed very tight.

Attracted by finely tuned chemical forces, two such monolayers come together so that the tails from both layers will also contact each other in a tail-to-tail arrangement. This automatic 3-D, multi-component packing ensures that the water-hating tails are hidden from water while the water-loving heads on the outer and inner surfaces are exposed to water. Water is therefore placed inside and outside the cell, but is helpfully expelled from the interior of the phospholipid membranes that enclose the aqueous cells.

Again, it's as if a causal power with foresight anticipated this need and engineered a perfect solution.

Phospholipids

THE CELL membrane needs to be elastic but at the same time also mechanically and chemically resistant so that it can continuously protect the cell from its fluctuating surroundings. Fortunately for life, phospholipid bilayers are flexible, but also highly stable, being resistant to mechanical stress and pH and temperature fluctuations.

So, how are all these properties obtained? By means of a fine, dynamic balance of the various physico-chemical properties of the many molecular constituents of the wall. (If the following explanation is too technical for your taste, feel free to skip down to this subsection's final paragraph. The summary there will give you enough to go on.)

The control of these chemical properties is accomplished primarily through regulation of the strength, length, and 3-D orientation of carbon-carbon bonds in the lipid tails. A carbon atom can form four bonds, including bonds with other carbon atoms. In lipids, such bonds can be single (C-C) or double (C=C). Single bonds are called "saturated" and double bonds are called "unsaturated." The side chains (R) attached to the two carbon atoms in a C=C bond can be on the same side (an arrangement called "cis": $^RC=C^R$), or on opposite sides (an arrangement called "trans": $^RC=C_R$).

Unsaturated phospholipids contain mainly cis $^RC=C^R$ bonds, which produce very pronounced and properly located bends in the long hydrocarbon chains. Cis unsaturated fats are less thermodynamically stable than their trans analogues, but the cis variety is still the blue-ribbon winner for this job, because the resulting kinks in the fatty acid chain lead to less packed aggregates than trans unsaturated lipids or saturated lipids. Cis unsaturated lipids have therefore lower melting points than saturated lipids or trans unsaturated lipids. The amazing result: membranes that can be made gradually more fluid.[5]

Shorter or longer carbon chains and different polar "heads" are also used to control the chemical properties of these molecules: an apparent master play of foresight guided by superb chemical wisdom.

Note that if we attribute the origin of biomembranes to blind material processes, we would need to appeal to a myriad of chemical "miracles." First, an accident would have to construct rather long carbon chains containing from twelve to eighteen carbon atoms. Such an accident is extraordinarily unlikely, statistically and chemically. Second, two of these chains would have to bind to a triol molecule—glycerine. Less stable cis $^RC=C^R$ bonds would also have to be inserted at the exact positions and in the proper ratio to produce the proper fluidity. A phosphate anion (PO_4^-) and another polar group, such as an ethylene diamine group, must also all be available at the same time and be properly connected to the final "molecular Lego" (Figure 1.2). As a chemist, I would never take this cascade of chemical miracles for granted.

Those specializing in prebiotic chemistry normally assume that rather primitive "entities" surrounded by primitive "membranes" with interiors very inhospitable to life, such as those of fatty acid micelles, were able to engulf a "primordial-RNA" molecule, giving rise to life on Earth.

As Sheref Mansy and his colleagues argue in a 2008 *Nature* article, "Fatty acids and their corresponding alcohols and glycerol monoesters are attractive candidates for the components of protocell membranes." The reason for this hope is that they do two crucial things. First, they form bilayer membrane sacs that retain small RNA molecules, and they can grow and divide,[6] which is essential if the primitive entity is going to be able to reproduce. This proposed pre-life entity supposedly jump-started the synthesis of life's first proteins.

But if this indeed happened, where did the amino acids needed for protein synthesis come from? They would have to come from outside, of course, from the "primordial soup" and migrate through channels into these "primordial cells." But at this point in the proposed scenario there aren't any membrane channels, so the amino acids would have to migrate through the "primordial membrane" itself to reach the cell's interior. But these primordial membranes would constitute an insuperable chemical barrier for amino acid permeation, so the hope is chemically impossible. If there is no route into the cell interior, then the cell dies in short order. No survival. No reproduction. No evolution.

So, again, the intimation of foresight is powerful. An exquisite phospholipid membrane for the cell apparently had to be anticipated, engineered, and made available just as the cell interior appeared on the scene, lest a skinless cell meet a swift, sure end. And since early cells obviously did survive, thrive, and reproduce, leaving offspring down to the present, it is scientifically plausible to conclude that by some means this extraordinary membrane did appear on the scene in that original moment of need. Some insist it was blind fortune. I disagree and urge us to consider a second possibility—engineering foresight.

Aquaporins: Water Filters Extraordinaire

LIPID BILAYER membranes protect and accommodate life, but as previously noted, the cell also needs channels to ferry essential materials in and out. If we had contracted out the job to a top nano-tech company employing all its powers of engineering foresight, we couldn't have been more pleased with the result. These lipid bilayer membranes come with 3-D protein assemblies that work beautifully as selective channels. These channels are smart enough to let in what needs to be let in and keep out what needs to be kept out.

For an evolutionary model of membrane origins to work, it must account for the co-evolution of membrane-associated proteins, membrane bioenergetics, and lipid bilayers[7]—a triple concatenated miracle. Attempts to wrestle with this question often begin with a confession of bafflement, as when A. Y. Mulkidjanian and his colleagues wrote that "the origin(s) of the membrane(s) and membrane proteins remains enigmatic."[8]

One thing membrane channels must permit is the passage of water. For this essential task biomembranes contain special channels called "aquaporins." Cells are cybernetic, multimolecular cities full of high-tech machines, power plants, and even nano-robots. But for all that nano-tech to properly work, it needs the same thing you and I need in large quantities—water. Indeed, this simple but essential and wondrous molecule, H_2O, with so many cellular functions, must be able to enter and exit the cell interior if the cell is to survive and thrive.

However, water entry and exit must be carefully controlled if the cell is to survive. This need for control arises because water molecules are connected by hydrogen bonds, and its hydrogen-bonding network makes water function as a "proton wire" that carries protons (H^+) down it, much as an electrical wire carries electrical current. But for metabolic reasons all cells must keep their interiors electrically negative. Cells manage this with special membrane channels that control the transport of sodium (Na^+) and potassium (K^+) ions. If aquaporins were to let water enter the cell freely, the "proton wires" would allow positively charged hydrogen ions (H^+) to overwhelm the cell's efforts to remain electronegative. So a simple water gate isn't enough.

This engineering challenge is no easy one to solve, even if you imagine an engineer with out-of-this-world powers. If such an engineer changed the intrinsic properties of the H_2O molecule to remove its proton-wire ability, this would muck up many of the other unusual and life-essential properties of H_2O. But happily, an ingenious solution was found that didn't require water to be re-engineered.

Aquaporins[9] in cell membranes not only let H_2O into and out of the cell, but also keep out impurities such as undesirable ions and other harmful biomolecules, as well as the positively charged hydrogen ions (H^+) that normally travel freely along H_2O's proton wires.

So how is this intricate task accomplished?[10] Let's take a look and see.

If what follows is overly technical for your tastes, feel free to skip down to the next subheading, where I summarize the discussion.

In the aquaporin water gates, a special amino acid known as asparagine is perfectly positioned, at the exact point of passage of a single H_2O molecule.[11] Asparagine is a member of the marvelous set of amino acids that are important for building and shaping the structures of proteins, but in addition it possesses a side group able to establish two very strong and spatially oriented H-bonds with H_2O molecules. The perfect 3-D alignment of this amino acid, perpendicular to the passage of the H_2O proton wire, then can function as a true "molecular plier" to cut the H_2O wire.

Here's how it works. Exactly at the moment it passes through the filter orifice, H_2O is twisted by asparagine. This exquisitely orchestrated maneuver, driven by stronger H-bonds, breaks the network of water's H-bonds, thereby cutting the H^+ wire. With a broken H^+ wire, H_2O freely enters the cell while its uninvited sidekick, H^+, is blocked at the door. Another life-or-death problem anticipated, and neutralized.

Aquaporin Power

AQUAPORINS, THEN, are an ingenious solution to a fiendishly tricky engineering problem. But in our uniform and repeated experience, ingenious engineering solutions are accomplished by geniuses—minds that apply expertise and foresight to a problem that couldn't be solved even by other engineers, much less by mindless natural forces.

So, was the cellular membrane's ingenious solution to the proton wire problem a work of blind fortune, or brilliant foresight? The discovery of this marvel of molecular ingenuity earned the 2003 Nobel Prize in Chemistry, "for the discovery of water channels" and "for structural and mechanistic studies of ion channels."[12] But if Nobel-caliber intelligence was required to figure out how this existing engineering marvel works, what was required to invent it in the first place?

The dominant explanation in origins biology involves some form of the random variation/natural selection mechanism, by which nature is said to have climbed the various Mount Improbables[13] we find in biology, one small mutational step at a time. Yes, there are additions and other adjustments to this basic mechanism in modern evolutionary theory, but these have significant shortcomings (see the final chapter). Also, dig long enough and you find some version of the chance/selection mechanism playing a key role in every leading model of biological origins. The problem is, natural selection can only go to work once a viable, self-reproducing cell exists, and it can only progress if each stage in the proposed evolutionary process of construction can somehow be preserved and passed along. Yet nothing gets preserved and passed along if the first proto-cells die a swift death for lack of a fully functioning cell membrane, able to accomplish the many essential tasks outlined above (among many others).

No multi-tasking cell membrane, no life. No life, no gradual evolution by random variation and natural selection. A hypothetical primitive membrane with a partly evolved aquaporin, one that allowed water in but hadn't yet evolved the ability to block the entry of H^+, would have no chance of survival. Such a cell, surrounded by the many enemies of a primordial ocean or "warm little pond," would quickly die. No survival. No reproduction.

The fully functioning H_2O-only gates (no H^+ allowed) are a "must" for any type of cell, from the most sophisticated to the most "rudimentary," if any such rudimentary cells ever existed on this planet. These highly selective and exquisitely engineered gates need to be there from the very beginning. No H^+-free water, no life.

And the proton-wire challenge, remember, is just one of the problems in need of a solution. An only partly evolved water gate with holes either too small or too big would either block water altogether or allow other contaminant molecules to enter the cell and destroy it. A successful water gate in this instance poses an "all or nothing" challenge for life. Foresee the need for these exquisitely precise water gates and somehow engineer them for just-in-time delivery, or the grand start-up called life quickly goes bust.

And what's true of the water gates is true of many other aspects of the cell membrane. If we are guided only by the evidence, this complex and multifaceted engineering marvel appears well out of reach of the random variation/natural selection mechanism. Another type of cause appears necessary, one that can foresee and engineer a cell membrane in all its marvelous sophistication, for just-in-time delivery.

And indeed, multi-faceted solutions of this sort, ones that anticipate problems that otherwise would stop any potential evolutionary development in its tracks, are evident throughout life. In the chapters that follow, we will look at many other spectacular examples.

2. A World Foreseen

for Biochemistry

STILL VIVIDLY REMEMBER THE FIRST TIME I SAW THE OCEAN. IT WAS in the '60s, during summer break. Time for fun, so my father drove our family of six in our Volkswagen Kombi van to Santos, a seashore in Brazil where Pelé used to play football. Our parents had told us so much about the ocean, and burning with anticipation, my brother, two sisters, and I kept asking from the back seat, "How long?" until at last we heard the waves and felt the salty breeze coming through the open windows.

We weren't yet to our destination, but my father, knowing how eager we were, pulled over at a spot close to the shore and stopped the Kombi so we could pile out of the van and take in the ocean for the first time.

Figure 2.1. When I got my first experience of the ocean as a boy, I was amazed by the wonders all around me. I remember asking myself, *Who did all of this?*

I will never forget that feeling: the smell of the sea, the blue sky and green water, the grainy sand under my feet, the warm sun on my skin, the water lapping my feet.

In that moment I was wide awake to the wonders of Earth. But Earth's wonders are with us every day; our eyes simply grow dim to them. Our planet is packed with marvels, from a transparent atmosphere to colorful rainbows, the aurora borealis, starry nights, birds, dragonflies and whales, sunrises, buzzing bees, and flowers great and small.

For a young kid, the first sight of some new vista of natural wonders is often unforgettable; but as we grow older we sometimes forget to keep contemplating, to keep seeing a world full of smells, textures, colors, and sounds, to keep appreciating the amazing things around us.

Science has helped me maintain into adulthood that sense of wonder. Absolute wonder and gratitude.

In the last chapter, we saw how the cell is carefully engineered with a lipid bilayer membrane and selective channels. These components are essential from the start. There would be no hope for a cell to become viable if it had to tinker around with mutations over thousands of generations in search of a functional membrane. It's anticipate or die. As we will see in the rest of the book, this need to anticipate is also true of numerous other systems and features throughout life, from the simplest cell to the function of the human body. The evidence of foresight is abundant, appearing almost everywhere you turn your eyes in biology.

There is also this: All of those marvels depend on deeper levels of foresight. Science has revealed that Earth and the cosmos display layer upon layer of features essential to life. It's a wondrous discovery, and it's the subject of this chapter.

Fine Tuning and Foresight

CURRENTLY, IT is believed there are at least twenty-six physical constants in the universe whose precise values must be carefully set to allow for life. These constants are things like the speed of light (c), the gravitational constant (G), and the Planck constant (h). All their values, uniquely suited to allow (though not cause) the amazing display of bio-chemistry we explore in this book, fall under an idea scientists call "fine tuning."

This fine tuning is commonly illustrated using a radio dial that needs to be set exactly at the correct frequency—"tuned"—to find the desired station. If the universe were a radio and the desired frequency allowed life, it would have dozens of dials for setting the values of the universal constants.[1] Muff even a single of these dial settings by even a tiny bit when first tuning the universe, and the result would be a universe with no life at all. For example, if the gravitational force were a little stronger than it actually is, stars would burn too quickly to function as stable providers of energy for life; a little weaker, and stars and planets would become unstable too quickly or never form in the first place.[2] Essentially, the laws and constants of physics are set to support life.

In examining some of the fine-tuned constants that had been dis-covered by the 1980s (and there have been many more discovered since then), physicist Fred Hoyle noted that they were so carefully tuned for life that they appeared to be "a fix," that is, planned. He was moved to conclude, "A common sense interpretation of the facts suggests that a superintellect has monkeyed with physics, as well as with chemistry and biology, and that there are no blind forces worth speaking about in nature."[3]

Note that Hoyle was not a religious man; he was an atheist. He simply recognized what many others have as well, including some of the world's leading physicists and astronomers: The fine tuning of the universe provides some of the most compelling evidence for a designing intelligence behind the cosmos.

Theoreticians hope to find a unified theory of everything, and some of those wishing to avoid the implication of design hope that such a dis-covery will decrease the number of such fundamental constants. If this occurs, however, those discovered super-constants, while less numerous, would necessarily be fine-tuned to an even more astonishing degree than the constants they subsumed.

So far, however, the trend has been in the opposite direction. The more that scientists learn about the universe, the more fine-tuned constants they discover for a life-sustaining universe. Let's look at just a few of these now.

Water: An Ideal Chemical Matrix

OUR EARTH is ideally suited in many ways to host life. With its carefully timed twenty-four-hour rotation, its large stabilizing moon, its location in the Milky Way's galactic habitable zone, its perfect distance from a special star, and its neighborly gas giant planets that protect it from many of space's dangers, Earth is curiously life-friendly.

But despite all these conditions, Earth still would have been unable to host life if it lacked special properties to allow biochemistry. For instance, its crucial solid crust could easily have been a desert, blazing hot during the day and freezing at night. Had this been the case, no careful tuning of distances, physical/chemical properties, or rotation period would have made a difference. Luckily, a marvelous molecule with dozens of unique properties provided Earth with a solution that perfectly anticipated this need: water.

For most of us, pure water, odorless and colorless, is easy to take for granted. But in fact it's a great chemical miracle. A myriad of properties and values of chemistry and physics had to be just so to make possible water and its many life-essential anomalies.

Also fortunate: Although liquid water is very elusive elsewhere in our solar system, Earth's surface has a significant amount of both land and liquid water on its surface—specifically, a 2:1 ratio of water to land.[4] This is a stroke of good fortune because liquid water is critical to life, and is the only liquid in a relatively narrow range of temperatures and pressures. This range is unimaginably narrow compared to the wide range of temperatures and pressures found in the universe, and yet they are exactly the ones present on Earth.

The solar system and beyond is indeed "awash in water,"[5] but mainly in solid or gaseous forms that do life little good. On Earth, however, we have water in all three states. And we need all three states for life to thrive here. If this need had not been anticipated, and Earth were typical of other planets in our galaxy, life could never have existed here.

Water's diverse set of chemical features solves many problems that would otherwise be dead-ends for life.[6] Its high specific heat moderates temperature changes between night and day, stabilizing the temperature by absorbing heat during the day and releasing it at night. The great amount of heat needed to evaporate water also helps us to cool down on hot summer days through evaporative cooling from our naked skin.

Water is not only crucial on Earth's surface and in the atmosphere. It is also crucial to the biochemistry of our bodies. Accounting for close to two-thirds of our body weight, water is so important to human functioning that we die in a matter of days from lack of it. It serves this crucial role thanks to many of its unusual properties. To give one example: Water is a relatively poor heat conductor, and this anomaly prevents organisms from boiling or freezing too easily.

Other unusual properties allow water to penetrate cell membranes, ascend via a strong capillary effect to the top of even very tall trees, and evaporate from the surface of leaves as needed, enabling plants to both transport nutrients and successfully conduct a myriad of biochemical operations.

The groundwork for these and many other life-essential properties of water appears to have been laid before water arose in the universe. These properties include:

- The specific masses and electrical charges of the neutrons, protons, and electrons that make up its H and O atoms.

- The precise strengths of the nuclear forces that stabilize protons and neutrons and hold them together in the nucleus.
- The precise strength of the electromagnetic force.
- The chemical rules and physical quantum laws that shape water's bonding and non-bonding molecular orbitals that hold pairs of the original electrons of both hydrogen (H) and oxygen (O) in specific energy levels in the H_2O molecule.
- The Pauli Exclusion Principle that limits to two the number of electrons in each of these molecular orbitals.
- The strength of the repulsion forces for bound and unbound pairs of the electrons that surround the central oxygen atom, a strength determined by a series of universal constants that directly and indirectly control the behavior of such atoms and the precise angle of the H-O-H configuration.

The list could go on and on. These many properties and values had to be precisely balanced—in advance—to create the dozens of exquisite anomalies of water that make life on Earth possible. It looks like it was planned ahead of time.

Water's properties are so weird that a paper in the prestigious journal *Nature* suggested that it has a sort of "memory"[7] that could be digitized, transmitted, and reinserted into another sample of water. Although water may not have "memory" *per se*, it does seem that something or someone capable of both memory and foresight is behind water's existence.

Water as Super-Solvent

Another striking chemical property of water that makes it so important to life on Earth is its ability to dissolve so many different substances, transporting all sorts of nutrients and waste products throughout—as well as in and out of—the cells of plants and animals.

Water is polar, meaning its electron density is not uniformly distributed around the molecule. One side is electron deficient (positive) and the other is electron-rich (negative). This polarization, together with the water molecule's size and ability to form hydrogen bonds, helps it dissolve amino acids, some peptides, hormones, globular proteins, and various other biomolecules, as well as inorganic salts. Although it doesn't dissolve every substance (very fortunately—see below), water dissolves more substances than any other liquid, such that it is sometimes referred to as "the universal solvent."

When we look at water's atomic makeup, we see another crucial level of beauty, sophistication, and chemical fine-tuning. The water molecule's three atoms are configured in an angular fashion (104.5°), and the H and O atoms have distinct electronegativities. These characteristics, taken together, make it a quite polar molecule with asymmetric electron density. This makes water great for solvating ions and moving these encapsulated ions around cells and the human body.

At the same time, water doesn't overdo its showy capacity to dissolve things. Happily for life, large biomolecules, such as fatty acids and the large proteins that make up the structure of our bodies, are insoluble in water. Good thing. This insolubility enables us to "sing in the rain" and to swim, bathe, and drink both hot tea and cold lemonade without being washed away due to water's near-universal solvency. We're up to two-thirds water. If water suddenly gained the capacity to dissolve these biomolecules, we would melt like the wicked witch at the end of *The Wizard of Oz*.

Rather than dissolving proteins, water helps them fold. This folding is aided by water's strong *dipole moment*. A dipole moment is created when a molecule's atoms share its electrons unequally. Water's unique dipole moment establishes its hydrogen bonds, while a specific H-O-H angle of 104.5° calibrates its polarity, allowing H_2O to establish strong hydrogen bonds with proteins. This chemical pulling enables nascent proteins to properly fold into specific and functional 3-D shapes, which are essential for their biological activity.

The Weirdness of Floating Ice

Due to the laws of physics, the solid state of a substance is almost always denser than its liquid state. There is, however, a major exception to the rule: water. Reaching maximum density at about 39°F (4°C), water is actually less dense when it is frozen. This anomalous feature allows water to circulate and revitalize water bodies on Earth, transporting noxious gases to the surface and oxygen to the bottom.

Consider the alternative. If ice didn't float, if it were denser than its liquid form—as is the case with the vast majority of liquids—lakes in cooler climates would freeze solid from the bottom up, jeopardizing the lake's life. The oceans would also freeze, not only at the poles where they now freeze, but on the ocean floors, and the freeze would extend much farther south and north from the poles—a devastating situation for marine life.[8]

Instead, ice expands when freezing, so it floats on top, preserving life. Life is preserved, therefore, because water likes to break rules. Ice is lighter (less dense) than liquid water, and is an unusually good thermal isolator. Together these two properties form an isolating ice cap that keeps lakes from freezing all the way to the bottom, so animals can keep living below the ice. It's a crazy solution to an inherent problem, but it is also very ingenious. If water ceased to be anomalous in these ways, life would be in serious trouble.

Let's consider another counterfactual scenario. Suppose water could remain a liquid far below 32°F and never froze within Earth's ambient temperature range. Then, water would lose most of its decorative properties—no more snow, no multitude of water crystal forms, no dreaming of a white Christmas, no wintertime sledding, and no majestic glaciers. What a loss!

But to understand how truly unique water is, you have to investigate it on the molecular level. The molecular weight (MW) of H_2O is 18 Daltons (Da). The MW of methane (CH_4) is quite close at 16 Da (only 2 Da less), but H_2O has remarkably high melting and boiling points (32°F and

212°F respectively) compared to CH_4 (-296.5°F and -258.9°F). H_2O also has a wide range of temperatures (spanning 180°F) where it can remain a liquid, compared to methane, which has a "liquid window" of just 37.6°F.

The energy required to vaporize liquid water is also over four times greater than for methane. Ice also requires a lot of energy to melt, heat, and then vaporize, allowing the oceans to store great quantities of heat. This is a big part of why the weather is so temperate in many coastal cities. The moisture in the water and in the air tends to smooth out big temperature swings.[9] In contrast, deserts, which of course are short on moisture, tend to see major temperature swings.

We've barely scratched the surface of water's anomalous, life-friendly properties. Given all of these, one of the most striking features of water is its chemical simplicity. It is a marvelously elegant molecule: H-O-H— just two of the smallest atom, ^1H, bonded to a single and also relatively light ^{16}O atom. How could this simple molecule be found to perform so many magic tricks and have so many weird properties? Water's simplicity is also an argument for design and foresight. It is often said that the use of simple things to achieve complex results is a mark of genius. As the French author George Sand put it, "Simplicity is the most difficult thing to secure in the world... the last effort of genius."[10] The humble H_2O molecule solves multiple complex problems for life on Earth with great simplicity.

The Perfect Atmosphere

OUR ATMOSPHERE is also amazing and necessary. Among other things, it protects us from bombardments from space. It filters out the dangerous radiation from the Sun while allowing crucial light through. And it moderates Earth's temperature.

Our atmosphere is made up of just the right gases in just the right proportions to support life on Earth: 21% oxygen (O_2), 78% nitrogen (N_2), and a little argon (Ar), carbon dioxide (CO_2), and water vapor (H_2O).

These gases are unreactive with each other—a crucial factor for long-term stability.

We know that O_2 is what we need to breathe to produce chemical energy in our bodies, so why are all those other gases necessary? An atmosphere with pure O_2 would be disastrous for life on Earth. Plants, which require carbon dioxide, would be impossible. Wildfires would rage uncontrollably. And even oxygen-breathers, including animals, would suffer from excess oxygen. Nitrogen (N_2) is a stable and rather unreactive gas that dilutes O_2 to a life-friendly proportion.

Earth's atmosphere also contains traces of other gases, such as Ar, CO_2 (from volcanoes), and CH_4 (from cattle). Though they are only present in tiny amounts, they are necessary to life, forming the perfect greenhouse effect for life to stay warm and have access to enough energy.

N_2 is also essential for life on Earth and is perfectly suited to be the major constituent of our atmosphere, since it creates an atmosphere sufficiently thick to stabilize the planet's liquid water and resist cosmic bombardment. N_2 is a highly stable, chemically inert molecule made of two tightly, triply bound $N \equiv N$ atoms, providing a perfect "solvent" for O_2. The final mixture has the right air pressure and density to facilitate breathing and destroy most debris from space. N_2 also provides nitrogen atoms for amino acids, the building blocks of proteins, and also for a wonderful array of other crucial nitrogen-containing biomolecules.

N_2 and O_2 are therefore both essential for life on Earth and in roughly the specific ratio they are found in our atmosphere.

Our N_2-plus-O_2 atmosphere is transparent to radio waves and visible light; hence we can appreciate that multitude of stars in the night sky while the atmosphere creates a blue sky during the daytime and a reddish sunset. This mixture of gases blocks the harmful radiation from the Sun even while letting us see so much of space, and send and receive radio waves. What an exquisite balance!

But even with such a superb atmosphere, there is remains a problem to solve: Animals would quickly consume O_2 and N_2, converting O_2 into CO_2 and burning up Earth from an excessive greenhouse effect. Earth also needed processes to systematically fix N_2 to the soil and oceans in a biochemically useful form. And indeed these processes are in place. A highly intricate network that includes lightning, microbes, plants, and animals creates the Earth's O_2 and N_2 cycles.[11]

If proper O_2 dilution and air pressure were the only major concerns, other gases could be selected, but the greenhouse effect of such gases would spoil the soup. Gases such as carbon dioxide (CO_2), water vapor (H_2O), methane (CH_4), and ozone (O_3), which are common in the atmosphere of other planets, could work as O_2 solvents, but high concentrations of them would trap too much heat.

Note another balance of Earth's atmosphere. If Earth had no atmosphere at all, like Mercury, too much heat would leak into space during the night, freezing any life. Venus has the opposite problem. It isn't as close to the Sun as its neighbor Mercury, but it is the hottest planet in our solar system because its atmosphere is almost exclusively CO_2. This causes an extreme greenhouse effect, resulting in an average temperature of 864°F. So, Mercury's atmosphere—too little. Venus's atmosphere—too much. Earth's—just right.

Ozone

I've saved for last the best example of the foresight evident in our atmosphere: the ozone layer.

The ozone layer displays an exquisite interplay of carefully crafted solutions. The Sun emits about 90% of its radiation in the visible and infrared (IR) range, perfect for life and photosynthesis. But the other 10% of sunlight is composed of different subsets of ultraviolet (UV) radiation, some of which is harmful and some of which is beneficial to life. For example, a little of UV-B is beneficial since it is required to produce bone-strengthening vitamin D, while some birds, insects, and mammals

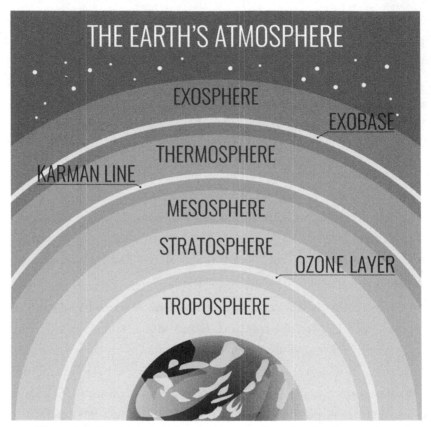

Figure 2.2. Earth's atmosphere protects us from bombardments from space. It filters out dangerous radiation and allows crucial light through. It moderates the temperature. And its recipe of gases is just the thing for life: 21% oxygen (O_2), 78% nitrogen (N_2), and a bit of argon (Ar), carbon dioxide (CO_2), and water vapor (H_2O).

can see UV-A and use it to hunt. UV rays are also used to treat some skin conditions, such as psoriasis, vitiligo, localized scleroderma, and atopic dermatitis.[12] But other portions of UV light are harmful.

The atmosphere is perfectly equipped to solve this "devil/angel" dilemma, blocking the great majority of the harmful stuff and letting the good stuff through. What is known as the ozone layer plays a crucial role here.

This atmospheric layer occupies the lower swath of the stratosphere, a portion stretching from nine to twenty-two miles above the Earth's surface. It isn't pure ozone, but it's richer in ozone (O_3) than are other parts of the atmosphere, containing a few parts per million of this essential triatomic molecule. The UV light emitted by the Sun is mainly composed of three subtypes: UV-A, UV-B, and UV-C, as well as a little UV-E. The ozone layer absorbs 97–99% of UV-B light, which would be potentially damaging to life in higher doses but provides a net benefit at lower doses. At the same time, it is mostly transparent to UV-A, the life-friendliest of the ultraviolet lights.

But what is really amazing about the O_3 layer is that it works in perfect synchrony with N_2 and O_2, forming an $O_2 + O \rightleftharpoons O_3$ perfectly balanced equilibrium mediated by both UV-C and UV-E radiation. The O_3 layer also seems to contain exactly the concentration at exactly the right altitude to block bad UV-C and excess UV-B radiation while letting UV-A and a useful amount of UV-B pass through.

O_3 also occurs in a layer close to the Earth's surface, but as the U.S. Environmental Protection Agency explains, we create that ozone through industrial "chemical reactions of oxides of nitrogen (NO_x) with volatile organic compounds (VOC) in the presence of sunlight," leading to urban smog. The main sources of NO_x and VOC are emissions from electrical utilities and industrial facilities, vehicle exhaust, gasoline vapors, and chemical solvents. O_3 is harmful to our lungs and damages crops, trees, and vegetation in general.[13]

The problem would be much worse if not for the fact that O_3 is a rather reactive molecule in the lower atmosphere, preventing it from accumulating to levels that would prove far more dangerous. And also fortunately, it is long-lived in the diluted (and colder) stratosphere where the O_3 layer resides. The naturally formed O_3, nine-plus miles above us, protects rather than harms us, thanks to its precise positioning.

Ozone is created there when the most harmful and energetic portion of the UV-C light strikes O_2. It is also amazing to discover that UV-C carries all the energy required to split the tightly covalently bonded O=O molecule into two O atoms. This highly reactive atomic oxygen then combines with molecular O_2 to yield O_3. This means that O_2 chemically blocks the harmful radiation (UV-C) while at the same time creating beneficial O_3 via a very reactive oxygen atom. This forms the protective O_3 layer that filters excess harmful UV-B. But remember that O_3 is by itself harmful to life, so it's a good thing these reactions occur high in the sky.

All this intricate cascade of reactions induced by radiation appears to have required careful planning to get everything right—gas densities, air pressures, temperatures, and reactivity—to limit this biologically harmful, pungent, and heavier-than-air O_3 molecule to the right altitude and the right amount in our atmosphere.

Let me explain in more detail how the whole process works and preserves life on Earth. O_2 very much needs O_3 as its wingman. O_2 blocks most UV-C but it lets most of the UV-B through—far too much for life on the ground. UV-B escapes from the first O_2 defender but is caught by the second, O_3. When UV-B reaches O_3 in the ozone layer, it is mostly absorbed, splitting O_3 back into O_2 and O. Hence, the excess of UV-B radiation is eliminated while at the same time turning O_3 into O_2, feeding the $O_2 + O \rightleftharpoons O_3$ equilibrium that is known as the ozone-oxygen cycle.

To review, this time with numbers: Most harmful UV-C is first blocked by O_2—specifically, the portion with wavelength of 100–200 nanometers. Any UV-C left over from O_2 is blocked by the O_3 layer (the UV-C with a wavelength of 200–280 nm), so the UV-C doesn't reach the ground. The shorter portion of the UV-C band is then used to break O_2 to O, forming O_3, which blocks most of the sunburn-causing UV-B (the UV-B of 280–315 nanometers in wavelength). The friendly UV-A (315–400 nm) is nearly transparent to both O_2 and O_3, and much of this less harmful, mostly beneficial light reaches the ground. Atmospheric N_2 is also part of the intricate blocking-filtering cycle, since N_2 blocks the most harmful UV-E (of wavelength 10–100 nanometers).

And remember, while the ozone layer does filter most of the UV-B, a beneficial portion of its longest wavelengths is transparent to O_3, reaching the surface, which our bodies use to produce vitamin D.

Thus, an intricate interplay of different UV-absorbing and UV-reacting proprieties of three gases (O_2, O_3, and N_2) in our atmosphere protects life. If the O_3 (plus O_2 plus N_2) layer were not there, overexposure to UV radiations would severely threaten life under the sun. The productivity of crops would be significantly reduced, and humans would experience suppressed immune systems, blindness, and a pandemic of skin cancer.[14]

Lightning: Surprisingly Important

BOTH N_2 ($N\equiv N$) and O_2 ($O=O$) tie up all their otherwise solitary electrons, meaning they are unavailable for reactions. This means no reaction would naturally occur between $N\equiv N$ and $O=O$. This lack of reactivity is an essential property of our stable atmosphere. But we do need NO, and then NO_2, to act on Earth's soil as the key ingredients for nitrates (NO_3^-) and nitrites (NO_2^-). And this N_2 consumption had to happen while still preserving the atmosphere, so recycling N_2 and O_2 cycles had to be promptly in place. How to solve this chemical paradox of needing both chemical stability and eventual reactivity? The solution: lightning.[15]

Lightning is a spectacular pyrotechnic show of light and sound and has always fascinated men. It is so awe-inspiring that humans throughout history have associated lightning with the anger of gods. Lightning is caused by sudden flows of electric charge between charged clouds or between the ground and a charged cloud. Lightning strikes on Earth happen an estimated fifty to a hundred times per second on average, well over a billion a year.[16]

Scientists still debate the exact mechanisms of lightning, but generally believe that water freezes in clouds at temperatures ranging from 5° F to −13° F, forming ice crystals that collide with water droplets. In the process the ice crystals become positively charged, and the slushy mix of ice and supercooled water becomes negatively charged. The lighter, positively charged ice crystals tend to accumulate near the top of clouds, and the heavier, negatively charged ice-water mix, near the bottom. When the charged cloud passes over the Earth, it induces an opposite charge in the Earth below, and a natural capacitor is formed. Eventually, a cloud-to-cloud or cloud-to-ground discharge occurs though the N_2 plus O_2 mixture that forms our atmosphere.[17]

In this way, lightning provides enough energy to break the triply-bonded (and thus hard to break) $N{\equiv}N$ molecule to form single, highly reactive nitrogen atoms. The nearly inert nitrogen molecules are thus turned into reactive nitrogen atoms in our troposphere.[18] The nascent nitrogen atoms react with $O{=}O$ to form $NO + O$, and NO is in turn rapidly oxidized to NO_2. It has been estimated that a flash of lightning produces about 4×10^{26} molecules of NO_x (NO plus NO_2), or about forty kilograms.

Next, all of the major atmospheric ions—N^+, $N_2{}^+$, O^+, $O_2{}^+$, and $NO_2{}^+$—rapidly transfer charge to NO to produce NO^+, so lightning's final product is NO^+.[19] Thunder clouds hold enormous amounts of electric energy—enough to overcome the high activation energy for the $N_2 + O_2$ reactions that makes NO and then NO_2 and on to $NO_2{}^-$ and $NO_3{}^-$ anions in the soil.

This cycle that lightning helps drive isn't just helpful. As David Fowler and his colleagues explain, "The global nitrogen cycle is central to the biogeochemistry of the Earth, with large natural flows of nitrogen from the atmosphere into terrestrial and marine ecosystems through biological nitrogen fixation," and back to the atmosphere.[20] Biological nitrogen fixation (BNF) and lightning, which reduce unreactive molecular N_2 into NH_3, $NO_2{}^-$, and $NO_3{}^-$ and then to N-containing chemicals, provide fixed-nitrogen forms that, again, as Fowler and his colleagues explain, are "subsequently transformed into a wide range of amino acids and oxidized compounds by micro-organisms, and finally returned to the atmosphere as molecular nitrogen through microbial denitrification in soils, fresh and marine waters and sediments." And as they further explain, emission of N_2O in the wake of denitrification "plays a key role in the radiative balance of the Earth and in the chemistry of the ozone layer in the stratosphere, where N_2O is destroyed by photolysis,"[21] a chemical process that breaks molecules into smaller units via light absorption.

Biological nitrogen fixation and the production of NO_x by lightning are the solution to sources of new reactive nitrogen in our biosphere. A steady supply of reactive nitrogen is crucial not just for agriculture but for all life forms. Although the quantity of reactive nitrogen from lightning is believed to be more than an order of magnitude smaller than that from biological nitrogen fixation today, lightning is a key player in the nitrogen cycle and is important for forming ozone and maintaining the oxidation capacity of the atmosphere.[22] Without lightning to make NO from the reaction of N_2 with O_2, there would be no life.

And keep in mind that clouds, the intricate properties of changing phases, and the charge separation for ice crystals all result from the strong chemical forces that hold H_2O molecules together, namely their polarity and unique H-bonding properties. In other words, we need both lightning and charged aqueous clouds with billions of kilowatts in electrical power, or again, no life.

Is It Science?

So, WE see that Earth and the laws and constants of physics and chemistry had to be fine-tuned in numerous ways to make life possible, with much of the fine tuning having occurred before life arrived on the scene. Before all the little details of biochemistry could be planned for our lives, chemistry and the universal constants had to be fine-tuned. This dimension of fine tuning suggests that foresight played a role in the very fabric of the universe.

To neutralize the design implications of all this apparent foresight at work, some have resorted to claiming there are innumerable other universes out there, all unobservable, and we just happened to get the right settings, whereas most other universes in the multiverse weren't so lucky.[23] The various multiverse proposals for explaining fine tuning have major problems.[24] A detailed discussion of those would take us beyond the scope of this book, but even bracketing off those concerns, there is this: The multiverse fails to explain a long and growing list of things in biology that appear to have required creative input on planet Earth after the origin of our universe. That is, the exquisite fine tuning in physics and chemistry that has been discovered in recent decades is a necessary but not a sufficient condition for biological life. Other, later forms of fine tuning were also required.[25]

All this fine tuning, taken together, suggests not merely foresight but astonishingly ingenious foresight. And the more we learn about this subject, the more compelling the evidence of foresight becomes.

However, whenever this argument is made, one complaint always arises: If foresight was involved in the fine tuning of the cosmos, then it must have been the foresight of a supernatural being, one who transcends the cosmos and its laws; hence, any conclusion of foresight doesn't count as science.

This complaint raises a fundamental question: How *is* science properly defined?

Contrary to popular perception, science is a diverse human activity and there are many different scientific methods.[26] There is overlap, of course, but there are also some important distinctives. For instance, laboratory or bench science, focusing on how things work now, employs one methodology. But the historical sciences, including origins science, draw on the methods of bench science but also on others, since origins science seeks to discover the cause of events in the past, events therefore not observable in the way one could, for instance, observe things in molecular biology using advanced microscopes.

Of course, there are also differences in methodology even among the experimental sciences, as for instance, between ecology and physics.

Accordingly, science has been defined by scientists and scientific societies in many overlapping but also, at times, competing ways. For instance, the Kansas Board of Education defined science as a human endeavor aimed to explain the natural world, though they added one sweeping restriction: It can only appeal to natural forces: "Science is restricted to explaining only the natural world, using only natural cause. This is because science currently has no tools to test explanations using non-natural (such as supernatural) causes."[27]

I would contest the claim that origins science has no means of testing explanations that appeal to intelligent causes, supernatural or otherwise. There's also this objection: If the above definition were *the* proper definition of science, only one worldview would be allowed in science: naturalism. And that biased restriction would mean that fine tuning and all the other evidence of apparent foresight in nature must be ignored or explained away, for instance by appealing to fanciful ideas such as a multiverse. But such a restriction betrays an impoverished view of science that excludes evidence just because it fails to match a desired conclusion.

There must be a better, more general definition for science. And indeed there is: *Science is a systematic and unbiased search for knowledge about nature.* Under this definition, we are free to think, investigate, doubt, and conclude based on whatever evidence we have. The underlying principles of science are freedom of thought and speech, guided by data collected using systematic methods. If science—the search for absolute truths[28] hidden within nature—is to be considered an unflinchingly truth-directed endeavor, reason and evidence must be the only constraints.

With this understanding in place, it becomes clear that investigating possible evidence for fine tuning, foresight, and intelligent design are valid scientific projects. Honest debates and dialogue among people involved in a free scientific search for knowledge is the driving force of science. We should follow the evidence no matter who finds it and no matter what the motivation of the person who conducted the search, and regardless of what it may tell us about reality. That's the only science worth doing.

With this general understanding, in the next chapter we will return to our investigation of biochemistry, unfettered by any question-begging rule. Like good detectives we will follow the trail of clues, refusing to rule out live options prematurely, guided only by reason and the accumulating evidence.

3. THE CODE OF LIFE

NOW THAT WE HAVE A CLEAR UNDERSTANDING OF HOW FORESIGHT was needed to make biochemistry possible in the first place, let's return to the cell.

The cell has its own sophisticated information-processing system, much like a computer. Computer programs require programmers, conscious agents with knowledge and foresight who can code the needed instructions, in the right sequence, to generate a functioning and information-rich program. Is there any reason to think that the information in cells also was programmed by a programmer rather than by random processes? Let's dive into the details and consider our options.

Foresight in DNA

THE CELL'S genetic information is a foundational and most ancient characteristic of life.[1] It is essential to how all living things on Earth are formed, move, and reproduce. Without it, no cellular organism would produce the biomolecules essential to life.

If matter evolved into living cells through purely blind processes, as evolutionary theory holds, then this information somehow was generated from matter and energy, through unguided natural processes. Origin-of-life theorists committed to a purely naturalistic account of life must therefore explain how both this genetic information and the cell's information processing system appeared virtually all at once, since such things, by their very nature, work in direct synergy and thus cannot evolve bit by bit.

This impossibility shouldn't be surprising, since the genetic information and the genetic code together include features like semantic logic and the meaningful ordering of characters—things not dictated by any laws of physics or chemistry.

The genome sequence of a cell is essentially an operating system, the code that specifies the cell's various genetic functions, affecting everything from the cellular chemistry and structure to replication machinery and timing. Because certain functions are shared by all forms of life, genomes are all similar to a considerable extent. For example, all mammals share more than 90% of their genomes.[2] It has been estimated that even life forms as distinctive as humans and bananas share 60% of their genetic information.[3] The unique portions are specific instructions for the varying needs of different genera and species.

Because it is so crucial to life on Earth, genetic information had to be transmitted and stored in a way that was as compact, efficient, and error-free as possible. This need presents a set of problems that had to be solved and implemented virtually simultaneously, so that molecules able to store and transmit genetic information were ready to go in the very first organism.

DNA (deoxyribonucleic acid) is made up of three classes of chemical. One is the phosphate anion PO_4^{3-}, with its four oxygen atoms distributed in a tetrahedral fashion around the phosphorous atom, producing a triple negative charge. Another is the five-membered cyclic sugar molecule—ribose—with four available OH linking sites. (DNA uses a special form of ribose called deoxyribose. Deoxyribose has an OH replaced with an H. We will discuss the differences between ribose and deoxyribose in a bit, and their importance, but for now I will talk in terms of ribose only.) The third class of chemical comprises four different kinds of stable, rigid, and heterocyclic bases, two purines and two pyrimidines, each with the ability to firmly attach to ribose via covalent bonds and to each other via two or three H-bonding "supramolecular" arms.

The attachments form ribose-plus-base "ribonucleotides" that turn out to be ideal for transmitting information. Why is that? Let's take it in stages. Some of what follows in this chapter gets pretty technical, but I've arranged things so that if you want to skip forward, you can get the gist of the arguments by reading the first paragraph or two of each subsection, the final couple of paragraphs of each subsection, and the chapter's concluding subsection. There are also several helpful illustrations along the way.

The Phosphate Anion

IF IT's to be viable, life's long-term storehouse of genetic information cannot break down in the presence of water. The hydrolysis problem, in other words, has to be solved in advance or life's information storehouse would dissolve as quickly as a sand castle struck by the incoming tide. How DNA meets this challenge is a wonder of engineering finesse.

DNA is what's known as a polymeric ester, composed of a very long phosphate (PO_4^{3-}) wire—the wire runs close to two meters in humans—interspersed with ribonucleotides. This molecular architecture is perfectly suited for DNA, as you will see.

The 3-D chemical structure of PO_4^{3-}, with four terminal O-atoms and three net charges, allows it to bind to two ribonucleotides (using two of these O^- atoms) while one of the extra O^- stays single-charged. If "R" represents a ribonucleotide, this can be written as $(R^1O)(R^2O)$ $P(=O)-O^-$.

This remaining negative charge at the end is in resonance with two oxygen atoms. That charge resonance is essential, since it stabilizes the DNA molecule against reaction with water (hydrolysis) by forming an electrical shield around the entire double helix. This encompassing electrical field also holds DNA inside the cell nucleus, preventing the precious DNA from escaping via membrane permeation. These properties make PO_4^{3-} the perfect link to construct a stable DNA macromolecule, bonded to the right sugars and bases, well protected against hydrolysis, and perfectly encapsulated inside the nuclear membrane.[4] This exqui-

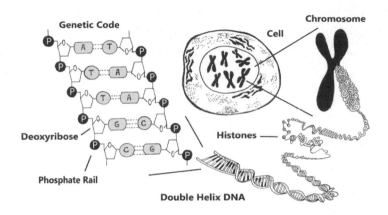

Figure 3.1. The DNA molecule is in the shape of a twisting ladder—a double helix. The phosphate side rails are on the outside, and the "rungs" of the ladder are the four nucleotides (A, T, C, G) that carry coded information. Histones serve as spools to package DNA into chromatin, the stuff of which chromosomes are made.

sitely engineered molecular arrangement, which protects DNA, had to be present for any cell to live. It's make or break.

For DNA to function properly, still another problem had to be solved. Inorganic PO_4^{3-} is the perfect link for DNA, but as a link for the long, polymeric molecule, its reaction with deoxyribose is too slow. The cell needed therefore a proper catalyst to speed up this slow but crucial reaction. Enzymes—large, exquisitely designed biomolecules—fulfill this task by accelerating the formation of such links by many orders of magnitude. Making enzymes is another whole incredible process we will discuss later. They would have been needed from the very beginning to make DNA. Yet they themselves have to be made using the DNA sequence they "were born" to make.

So we have two ingenious solutions to do-or-die challenges: an engineering marvel—an electrical shield—that protects DNA from breaking down in the presence of water; and another engineering marvel—enzymes—that speeds a crucial reaction that would otherwise be far too slow. And these two ingenious solutions could not come one after the other, because the DNA sequence is necessary to making the enzyme, while the enzyme is necessary for making the DNA. Both the polymeric DNA, with its multiple phosphate-sugar bonds and very slow kinetics, and the proper enzymes to accelerate the formation of the DNA phosphate-sugar bonds, have to be in place at the same time. If only one exists without the other, no cell at all.

Ribose

ANOTHER BIT of engineering cleverness was needed to cinch the stability of DNA. When forming the phosphate wire, PO_4^{3-} should be able to react with ribose at any of its four OH groups extending from the sugar molecule; but the intrinsic nature of the phosphodiester bonds found in DNA make exclusive use of 5'-3' OH groups. (As the ribose molecules in Figure 3.2 indicate, biochemists number the carbon atoms in them. The phosphate backbone of DNA binds the 5' carbon in one sugar to the 3' carbon in the next.) It turns out that this 5'-3' selectivity in OH binding increases DNA's stability when compared to 5'-2' linkages.[5] In DNA the 2' OH group is replaced by H, and is unavailable for binding, and for good reason. This change prevents hydrolysis of the DNA, which is essential for any molecule used for long-term storage of information.

A recent article expanded on the criteria for selection:

> The reason that nature really chose phosphate is due to interplay between two counteracting effects: on the one hand, phosphates are negatively charged and the resulting charge-charge repulsion with the attacking nucleophile contributes to the very high barrier for hydrolysis, making phosphate esters among the most inert compounds known... [But] the same charge-charge repulsion that makes phosphate ester hydrolysis so unfavorable also makes it possible to regulate, by exploiting the electrostatics. This means that phosphate ester hydrolysis can not only be turned on, but also be turned off, by fine tuning the electrostatic environment... This makes phosphate esters the ideal compounds to facilitate life as we know it.[6]

Thus, only phosphates have the dual capacity needed to make DNA work.

Researchers have constructed DNA analogues using sugars beside ribose and measured their properties. So was ribose, this very specific five-membered cyclic sugar, just one good option out of many? It appears not.[7] The final molecule had to be both stable and capable of carrying the code of life. For these jobs, only ribose will do. DNA analogues using other sugars are not suitable information storage molecules. Some DNA made of the other sugars fails to form stable double helices, or their intermolecular interactions are too strong or too weak, or their associations are insufficiently selective. Other DNA analogues adopt various conformations that would hinder the cell machinery from replicating them. Effectively, ribose was the only choice that would work.

Darwin suggested that life emerged by chance in a "warm little pond." In other words, an accident formed a masterful information-storage molecule equipped with the only sugar that could make it work. But judging from the myriad of molecules bearing two OH groups that could mimic it, the task of making, finding, and specifically selecting this particular and life-essential sugar at random in the "primordial soup" would be dauntingly improbable.[8]

Ribose is also ideal at forming a 3-D molecular structure. True, it is not the only sugar that allows for DNA to form a stable double helix, but it's far and away the best. The resulting inner space within the double helix is about 25 Å, and this distance is just perfect for one monocyclic nitrogen base (T or C) and one bicyclic base (A or G). This perfect space allows the formation of base pairs, in which (as we shall see below) A pairs with T and C pairs with G, forming a crucial selective criteria of the genetic code. If any sugar other than ribose were used, that distance would be too wide or too narrow.

DNA's Four Bases

ANOTHER CRUCIAL question: Why did life "choose" the very specific ATGC quartet of N bases? Another indication of the planning involved in the DNA chemical architecture arises from the choice of a four-character alphabet used for coding units three characters long. Why not more alphabetic characters, or longer units? Some of my fellow scientists are working on precisely such genetic Frankensteins. It's fascinating work. But DNA should be as economical as possible, and for DNA to last, it had to be highly stable chemically. And these four bases are exactly what are needed. They are highly stable and can bind to ribose via strong covalent N-O bonds that are very secure. Each base of this "Fantastic Four" can establish perfect matchings with precise molecular recognition through supramolecular H-bonds. The members of the G≡C pair align precisely to establish three strong, supramolecular hydrogen bonds. The A=T pair align to form two hydrogen bonds. A and G do not work, and neither do C and T, or C and A, or G and T. Only G≡C and A=T work.

But why don't we see G≡G, C≡C, A=A or T=T pairings? After all, such pairs could also form two or three hydrogen bonds. The reason is that the 25 Å space between the two strands of the double helix cannot accommodate pairing between the two large (bicyclic) bases A and G, and the two small (monocyclic) bases T and C would be too far apart to form hydrogen bonds.[9]

A stable double helix formed by the perfect phosphate-ribose polymeric wire, with proper internal space in which to accommodate either A=T or G≡C couplings with either two or three H-bonds is necessary to code for life. And fortunately, that is precisely what we have.

Ribose for RNA and Deoxyribose for DNA

THERE IS an even more striking example of potential problems in the DNA structure that had to be solved in advance. DNA must be highly stable, while RNA, as the temporary intermediate between DNA and protein (as we shall see below) must be dramatically less stable. RNA uses the intact ribose sugar molecule to make its polymeric wire, while DNA uses a de-oxygenated version of it—deoxyribose. Since an OH group has been replaced by an H at an apparently "chemically silent" 2'-position in the ribose ring, it seems strange at first sight to note such care for a seemingly trivial molecular detail. But it turns out that there is a crucial-for-life reason for this amazing chemical trick.

The choice of D-ribose for m-RNA and D-deoxyribose for DNA increases the chemical stability of DNA while decreasing that of RNA in an alkaline medium. Both of these are for a reason.

If nuclear DNA is the hard drive of life, storing information for the long term, messenger RNA (m-RNA) is life's flash drive, transmitting information over short periods of time. RNA's lifetime had therefore to be short, otherwise protein production would never stop. Life needed a way to quickly "digest" via hydrolysis and ideally recycle the components of RNA when its job is finished. When chemists analyzed this "mysterious" OH/H exchange, they discovered that the apparently "silent" 2'-OH group helps RNA undergo hydrolysis about one hundred times faster than DNA.[10] So we see that ribose had to be used in RNA for easy digestion in an alkaline medium, and deoxyribose had to be used

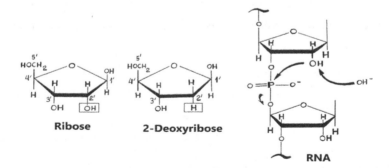

Figure 3.2. The chemical structures of ribose and 2-deoxyribose, and two ribose molecules linked to form RNA. The nature of the bond between two ribose molecules (as opposed to two deoxyribose molecules) diminishes the lifetime of RNA, which is actually crucial to life's information-processing system.

in DNA for longevity. Otherwise, life would be impossible. Again, by all appearances this stability control for both DNA and RNA had to be anticipated ahead of time and the solution provided with just-in-time delivery.

Homochirality and the U-to-T Exchange

THERE ARE other striking solutions within DNA and RNA. Like many other organic molecules, ribose can come in either a right-handed (D) or left-handed (L) form, and a random assemblage of the stuff would have a roughly equal mix of the two—what is known as a racemic mixture. But a racemic mixture of D-ribose and L-ribose would be biologically disastrous, rendering impossible the proper 3-D coherence of the double helix. Both DNA and RNA need either all D forms, or all L forms—not a mixture.

So here's the mystery: How could purely blind chemical forces have accomplished this challenging 3-D selection? Commenting on the puzzle, Philip Ball, a science writer and an editor of the journal *Nature*, once conceded, "On the 60th anniversary of the double helix, we should admit that we don't fully understand how evolution works at the molecular level."[11] That's putting it mildly.

There is another crucial difference between RNA and DNA. Where DNA uses thymine (T) as one of its bases, RNA uses uracil (U). This U-to-T exchange is intriguing because the chemical structures of T and U are nearly identical, distinguished only by a single, small methyl group (CH_3). As the editors of the *NSTA WebNews Digest* noted, converting uracil to thymine requires energy, so why do cells bother to methylate uracil into thymine for DNA?[12] Additionally, the extra group is placed in what seems to be a rather inert position on the T ring. It seems therefore that such a rather small and inert CH_3 group is there only to "differentiate" U and T while disturbing the chemical properties as little as possible. A number of evolutionary explanations have been offered for this U-to-T exchange,[13] but it turns out this exchange maintains the integrity of the whole information storage system, so a fully evolved form of it would have been needed from the start.

As we saw earlier, the four RNA bases—A, U, G, and C—are superb for the job they have, but they also cause a problem if used in the wrong context. The U-to-T exchange is the solution. The original quartet is fine for less stable RNA, but not the best choice for long-lasting DNA.

The U base would still establish preferential pairing with A, but the A=U pair is not ideal for the role DNA fills, since U can also match efficiently with all the other bases, including itself. DNA's T, on the other hand, is much more selective than U in its pairing with adenine (A), forming a more stable A=T pair. This specificity makes sense when you remember that DNA, which is made of nucleic acids, phosphate anions, and sugar molecules, is very hydrophilic (water-loving). As Michael Onken explains, the addition of a hydrophobic CH_3 group to U (thus forming T) causes T to repel the rest of the DNA. This, in turn, shifts T to a specific location in the helix. This perfect positioning causes T to bind exclusively with A, making DNA a better, more accurate information replication system.[14] This guarantees the long-lasting integrity of DNA information.[15]

So we see that the most fundamental design principles of the DNA helix are carefully tuned for the code to work properly, from the number of H-bonds between the A=T and G≡C interactions, to the exact fit of the molecules between the two wires that form the double helix.

Another Enzyme Wunderkind to the Rescue

BUT THERE is at least one other potential problem that could ruin the elegant logic of life's genetic code. Cytosine (C) is not as stable as the other bases, and as the time goes by, it degrades by deamination. When it degrades, it forms what? The U base. This degradation, of course, would corrupt the information by creating alien U's that shouldn't be there. RNA, because it is rapidly used and recycled within the cell, is immune to this aging problem. But DNA, with its much longer lifetime, can't use U. Without the U-to-T exchange, as well as U-to-C repair, this degeneration of C into U would be catastrophic to life.

It is because of this C-to-U degradation that DNA had to find a replacement for U. Degradation of C into alien U would be disastrous if it hung around in DNA. The alien U must be converted back into C. Enter uracil DNA glycosylase,[16] a repair enzyme specifically equipped to correct what would otherwise be a deadly software bug. This exquisite enzyme repairs all U's to C's. This repair works to correct the C-to-U errors, but imagine an "evolving scenario" in which the repair system was working but DNA used U instead of T. In it, the repair enzyme, not knowing the difference, would catastrophically repair everything back to C, including the bases that were supposed to be U. So both the U-to-T exchange and the U-to-C correction machine are necessary at once to preserve the information in DNA.

This correction machine scans the DNA, detects every alien U, and replaces it with a C. Cytosine degrades into uracil one thousand to ten thousand times a day—and that's in just one cell. But it never gets ahead of uracil DNA glycosylase, returning the DNA to its original and proper sequence.[17] The U-to-C correction machine is a work of pure genius.

The U-to-T exchange is not just a nice advantage, but a necessary function that had to be in place from the start. (If DNA were "born" using UU, its real U would be confused with the alien U formed by aging Cs. DNA glycosylase, if accidentally present, would not do any good, since then it would replace all U with a C, rapidly corrupting the information in DNA.) This amazing chemical trick is an insurmountable barrier for unguided evolution.

Take, for example, one popular origin-of-life theory: the RNA World. In this theory, life began with RNA,[18] which at some point invented DNA and was replaced by it. But supposing that this proto-DNA was made by the same RNA bases (and sugar), using U (and intact ribose), it would undergo hydrolysis too quickly, and the C-to-U degradation would corrupt DNA. Even if by some miraculous stroke of good fortune the U-to-T exchange happened to occur, the newborn DNA created by RNA would lack the enzyme repair mechanism to convert every alien U back into C, quickly killing the incipient life.

No second generation. No natural selection. DNA construction is an all or nothing affair.

Evolution may, at some point, have been granted a single wildly improbable stroke of good luck. But two simultaneous and synchronized such strokes of good fortune? That seems like a bridge too far. And multiple such strokes of good fortune are needed simultaneously: the PO_4^{3-} anion, the proper sugar (ribose), the correct bases ATGC, the U-to-T exchange, the OH/H exchange, and a homochiral D-ribose.

Genetic Redundancy

IN ADDITION to referring to the DNA sequences that contain information for synthesizing entire proteins, the term "genetic code" also can mean the set of rules that matches an amino acid to a specific DNA triplet (a combination of three nucleotides called a "codon"). The genetic code in this second sense features yet another hallmark of foresight and sound engineering: *redundancy*.

This redundancy is possible due to the genetic code's basic architecture, in which each of the three "letters" in a nucleotide triplet in sequence can be any of four different alphabetic characters, yielding 4 x 4 x 4 total possibilities—sixty-four all together. But there are sixty-four possibilities and only twenty amino acids. That leaves a lot of room for possible redundancies. In other words, more than one three-letter combination might code for a given amino acid, and that's in fact what we find.

This "redundancy" was initially interpreted as an inefficient artifact of evolution's sometimes messy trial-and-error process. At first, scientists thought that only twenty codons were needed for the amino acids, plus two more codons to signal the start and stop of protein synthesis

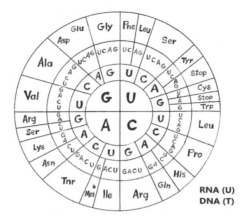

Figure 3.3. The genetic code with its "redundancy" of sixty-four codons for twenty amino acids. RNA uses uracil (U) whereas DNA uses thymine (T).

(called "translation"). Since then, however, we have discovered that the redundancy is actually vital. The apparent overkill minimizes reading and transmitting errors so that the same amino acid is transferred to each generation.

But if carefully inspected, the redundancies themselves don't seem to be random, since they involve mainly changes in the third letter of each triplet. For example, the simplest amino acid, glycine, has four codons that specify it: GGA, GGC, GGG, and GGT. The only position that varies is the third, and any nucleotide in that position will still specify glycine. (There are other biological effects possible, though—for example effects on the speed of protein synthesis and folding. See below.)

Changes in the first and second letters are less common, and are offset by the expression of amino acids with chemically similar properties and that don't significantly alter the structure and properties of the final protein. For example, the CTT codon that codes for leucine becomes the chemically similar isoleucine when the C is replaced by A (ATT). Such redundancies establish a chemical buffer between amino acids when common errors occur. That is, the code of life has built-in safeguards against potentially damaging genetic typos.

But that's not the only purpose of the redundancy in our genetic code.[19] The use of different codons to express a single amino acid also allows the speed of protein synthesis to be controlled. For example, four different codons may specify the same amino acid, but the four differ in their effects on how fast or slow a bond is made and the protein folds.[20] This kinetic control gives each protein the exact amount of time it needs to form the correct 3-D shape.

There are other nuances in our genetic code that seem to suggest foresight, such as the grouping of codons for amino acids with either acid or alkaline side chains.[21] Hence, if environmental stimuli require exchanging an alkaline (basic) amino acid for an acidic amino acid in a protein, this exchange is aided by such grouping. Again, what a wonderful chemical trick! For example, a basic lysine coded by either AAA or AAG can easily be changed to the acidic glutamic acid by only a single-letter substitution: GAA or GAG. Having such a flexible code helps the organism to stay alive.

The code also anticipates and has safeguards against the most common single-point mutations. For instance, leucine is encoded by no less than six codons. The CTT codon encodes leucine, but all the third-letter-mutation variations—CTC, CTA and CTG—are "synonymous" and also encode leucine.

First-letter mutations are rarer, and potentially more dangerous because they do change the amino acid specified—if C is exchanged for T, forming the TTT codon, a different amino acid (phenylalanine) will be expressed. But even for this, the genetic code has a safeguard: phenylalanine's chemical properties are similar to leucine's, so the protein will still retain its shape and function. If the first letter C in CTT (leucine) is replaced by A or G, something similar happens, since ATT (isoleucine) and GTT (valine) have physicochemical properties similar to leucine as well.

The 2015 Nobel Prize in Chemistry was awarded jointly to Tomas Lindahl, Paul Modrich, and Aziz Sancar "for having mapped, at a molecular level, how cells repair damaged DNA and safeguard the genetic information."[22] The 2016 Prize went to Jean-Pierre Sauvage, Sir J. Fraser Stoddart, and Bernard L. Feringa "for the design and synthesis of molecular machines," including "a tiny lift, artificial muscles, and minuscule motors."[23] That is, these six scientists uncovered the mechanisms of DNA typo corrections and produced nanomachines like the ones that repair the C-to-U degradation in DNA. Unravelling these processes took six of the most brilliant minds in chemistry, along with an army of other research groups, toiling for decades to lay the groundwork for these breakthroughs.

This *tour de force* of research and engineering sophistication thoroughly deserved two consecutive Nobel prizes. Are we then to believe that the marvels of engineering that these brilliant scientists discovered were themselves produced by a mindless process? If discovering the function of these engineering marvels took genius, how much more genius would be needed to create them?

The problem for evolutionary theory is exacerbated by the fact that evolution only works one step at a time. So, which came first, the DNA or the correction machinery? The correction machinery is encoded in DNA, but the DNA can only survive from generation to generation with the help of the correction machinery. It seems to be a chicken-and-egg problem for evolution.

Amino Esters and Ribosomes

DNA's FOUR-CHARACTER alphabet is used to compose the larger twenty-character alphabet of alpha amino acids (α-amino acids). Life needs this collection of twenty building blocks, each distinct, to make a protein. These building blocks must react with each other to form specific chemical connections called peptide bonds. Chemists have learned to use this reaction to make polymers like nylon, for which they used H_2N-$(CH_2)_6$-$COOH$ molecules as the specific building blocks. The reaction occurs without much guidance because NH_2 has no option but to react with $COOH$.

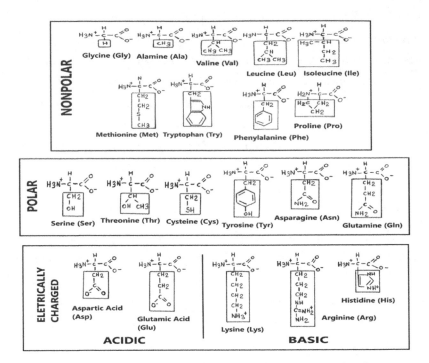

Figure 3.4. The 20 α-L-Amino acids, masterfully engineered to form a comprehensive yet economical set of building blocks for the proteins of life, displaying a range of all major intermolecular forces, from London dispersion forces of nonpolar carbon chains to H-bonding and charge attraction, as well as acid and alkaline properties.

It's much more complicated for proteins, however, since α-amino acids have twenty different side chains (called "R groups"; see Figure 3.4) attached to their backbones. Each protein is a polymer, a chain made of many subunits linked together like nylon, but composed of amino acids. But the amino acid R groups pose a serious problem for protein synthesis, because they can react favorably with both themselves and the COOH and NH_2 groups of the other α-amino acids. The desired peptide reactions, on the other hand, are usually unfavorable, requiring a positive change in free energy (abbreviated ΔG).[24] All the other viable side reactions will interfere with the formation of a protein polymer. So how does life get around this severe competition problem? Life relies on a chemical trick often used in synthetic chemistry: derivatization.

What follows gets pretty technical. Feel free to simply review the illustrations and then skip to the payoff, laid out in the final paragraph of this subsection.

Ribosomes are large multimolecular machines that synthesize proteins from amino acids in living cells. But before going to ribosomes, each α-amino acid is converted into an amino ester, a process called "derivatization," and attached to a "transfer RNA" (tRNA) by an enzyme called a t-RNA synthetase. There are distinct tRNAs and tRNA synthetases for each amino acid. Competition from energetically more favorable R-with-R or even R-with-NH_2 or R-with-COOH reactions would be fatal to protein synthesis if it were not for the ribosome. Here's what happens during the process of translation, as α-amino acids get attached to their specific t-RNA by their specific t-RNA synthetases. In a very elegant and ingenious process, amino esters are first phosphorylated by ATP and then, via a trans-esterification reaction, a t-RNA linked amino ester is formed.

To ensure the desirable NH_2-with-COOH reaction takes place, the amino acids are first esterified (which makes the chemical bond easier to form), then brought together by the mechanical hands of a ribosome, holding them in the correct position to prevent competing R reactions from taking place, and providing the necessary energy for the bond to form.

Again, this ribosome-driven reaction does not seem to be an advantage that life could acquire little by little, by trial and error. Chemically, it is impossible to produce a functional protein without ribosomes that have already solved the competing reaction problem, or without the collection of twenty specific tRNAs and tRNA synthetases that would feed it with amino esters. As in so many other cases with the cell and its code, if this need is not foreseen and planned for, there will be no cell at all.

Conclusion: Codes and Coders

Now LET'S step back a moment and review, focusing just on DNA. With its double-helix structure, DNA is the most efficient, most protected, best calibrated in terms of chemical stability, and most compact form of information storage known on the planet. How did this perfect, polymeric, nearly two-meter long, 3.2 billion-piece (for humans) molecular wonder form without anything telling it to? A cell doesn't know that only ribose will work, or that it needs an intact D-ribose for RNA but a D-deoxyribose for DNA, or a U/T exchange, or four bases with perfect fittings and sizes, or a stable and protective phosphate anion wire, or an electric shield, and more. And yet it has all these things and, indeed, it must have had them from the very first cell.

Antony Flew, a famous atheist philosopher who converted to theism late in his life after studying this evidence, concluded, "Fifty years of DNA research have provided materials for a new and enormously powerful argument to design."[25]

Morse code was created by an intelligent mind, that of Samuel F. B. Morse. The barcode was invented by the brilliant Norman Joseph Woodland, and the ASCII code by the visionary Robert Bemer. Codes always have code-makers.

DNA, RNA, and the genetic code (in the sense of sequences needed for protein synthesis) serve as beautiful examples of foresight, in their coordinated structure, maintenance, and back-up plans. Francis Crick, co-discoverer of the double helix, proposed a "frozen accident" scenario for the evolution of the genetic code,[26] but he was unable to fill in all the many details of this hypothetical accident, and fifty years later, naturalistic explanations for the origin of the code of life have not been forthcoming.

The genetic code dwarfs any human code in its sophistication and capacities. That by itself should be enough to suggest the possibility of foresight and design. But there's more. As it turns out, the genetic code cannot read itself or implement the instructions it holds. To do that, other sophisticated solutions are necessary. We investigate those additional tricks in the next chapter.

4. Life's Helpers

As we saw in the last chapter, the code of life is fantastically sophisticated, and it had to be carefully designed to function properly. But having a code isn't enough. You need a lot of helpers as well. In this chapter, we're going to examine some molecular machines that help turn DNA into proteins, and proteins into living things.

Operons

From the moment life is up and running, it needs a control mechanism to produce the right proteins at the right time at the right concentration. Cells need to be able to turn gene expression on and off to respond to environmental changes. Bacteria are a good example. As they encounter changing environments, bacteria express different enzymes (enzymes are a type of protein) depending on what nutrients are available. The bacteria can, for example, turn off genes that express lactose-metabolizing enzymes when they don't need them, and then turn these genes back on if lactose, the disaccharide in breast milk, suddenly becomes the only nutrient available. If glucose, the most preferred sugar, is present along with lactose, bacteria can even differentiate this detail and digest the glucose first before turning on the genes to digest lactose. In bacteria, this control is usually done with operons.

These clusters of co-regulated genes control protein synthesis. For example, the genes required to use lactose as an energy source are organized into the lactose operon, or "*lac* operon." This operon comprises three genes grouped together. The first gene, *lacZ*, encodes an enzyme that splits lactose into glucose and galactose (β-galactosidase). The second gene, *lacY*, encodes a "permease" needed to facilitate lactose up-take by the cell. And *lacA* is the third gene, required for using similar galactoside sugars. All three genes turn on or off in tandem. This clever grouping of genes under a common control mechanism allows a bacterium to quickly change its diet multiple times over the course of its life.[1]

This is now the stuff of high school biology textbooks; but when this mechanism was dissected in the 1960s, it actually provided the first understanding of gene regulation at the molecular level—resulting in Nobel prizes for the investigators. The steps in gene regulation even in the simplest organisms were impressive.

Evidence suggests that operons are ancient, and have always been a feature of bacterial chromosomes. Under a Darwinian view such organization is surprising: How is it possible for genes to evolve at random to then be recruited, juxtaposed on the chromosome, and assembled into operons so early in life's history?

An operon is made up of an operator, a promoter, and structural genes. (On some accountings an operon also includes a closely associated regulatory gene, which is the *lacI* gene for the lac operon.[2]) The genes are transcribed into messenger RNA (mRNA) by the protein called RNA polymerase, which normally begins the process of gene expression by binding to a promoter. However, there is an operator, a regulatory sequence in the DNA overlapping the gene's promoter DNA sequence. If a repressor protein, such as LacI, binds to the operator, it prevents the binding of the RNA polymerase to the promoter sequence. This binding in turn prevents transcription (*gene expression* is another way to say it) so that the gene's product (e.g., LacZ, LacY, or LacA) will not be made when lactose is absent from the environment, or present in combination with glucose. This mechanism ensures conservation of cellular resources by allowing gene expression only under the appropriate circumstances.

If the enzymes produced by the structural genes are actually needed, then the repressor is inactivated (removed from the operator), allowing RNA polymerase access to the promoter to initiate transcription. This is what's known as the induction phase.

In bacteria, which lack a nucleus, once mRNAs are initiated, ribosomes can immediately load on the messenger and start making protein even before the mRNA is completed. This coupling of transcription and translation in bacteria provides incredibly short response times to changing environmental conditions. When lactose suddenly becomes available, E. coli rapidly go from having only a few molecules of LacZ (β-galactosidase) in the cytoplasm to having 15% of its total cellular protein made of this enzyme.

James Shapiro offers the following observation in the journal Gene:

> A series of highly integrated molecular interactions allows E.coli cells to distinguish between two sugars and execute the following non-trivial algorithm: IF lactose is available AND IF glucose is not available AND IF the cell can synthesize beta-galactosidase and lactose permease, THEN transcribe lacZYA from the lac promoter.[3]

So we find that E. coli uses logic statements to make decisions, much like the logic statements used in computer coding.

The Sound of One Hand Assembling

PROTEINS ARE made from alpha amino acids that react to form a myriad of polymers (macromolecules consisting of many similar subunits). Most proteins must fold themselves into a functional 3-D shape. How does a mindless polymer know what to do? If it doesn't fold right, the protein can become deformed and broken. Proper folding requires a highly intricate balance of intra- and inter-molecular forces.

There are land mines all along the way to disrupt the exquisite choreography of protein folding. Fortunately, all of these were properly anticipated and defused.

Amino acids, if generated "at random," would come in two forms: right-handed (D) and left-handed (L) (see Figure 4.1), in what is called a "racemic mixture." The problem is that a racemic mixture would make a mess of the 3-D structure of a protein. If the cell were to use any but a

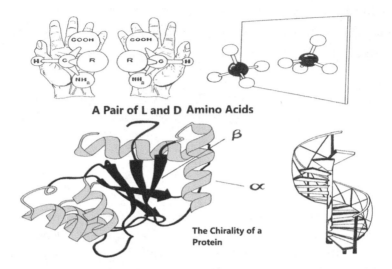

A Pair of L and D Amino Acids

The Chirality of a Protein

Figure 4.1. In the making of the self-folding, intricately curled proteins essential for life, only alpha-L-amino acids were used as the building blocks. This is fortunate because a mix of left- and right-handed wouldn't have worked. Interestingly, blind chemical forces tend to yield a roughly even mix of left and right, but somehow life was gifted with all lefties to work with. To get all lefties, we need a skilled biochemist or a living cell, but according to evolutionists, life is supposed to have gotten its start without either.

pure set of left-handed amino acids, or a pure set of right-handed amino acids, it could not produce a functional 3-D structure for a protein.

One possible solution to the L/D mixture problem would be to program DNA sequences for specific L or D amino acids. But this extra programming would be tremendously expensive, since extra codons for either L or D would be needed. Life exhibits a more elegant solution, having started with 100% left-handed amino acids—a situation referred to as *homochirality*.

If life started with a primordial soup, this means that right-handed alpha amino acids were somehow removed from—or kept out of—the primordial soup. This solution was a master stroke—and a most fortunate one for us. Without homochirality for the cell's amino acids, no functional protein would be feasible, and the cell would die. More precisely, it would never come to life.

Enzymes

LIFE REQUIRES quick execution of countless chemical reactions, which constantly occur at high speeds throughout our cells. To pull this off, incredible nanomolecular machines are required: proteins known as *enzymes* (Figure 4.2). These molecular wunderkinds, loaded with sophisticated chemical technology, are essential to accelerate many of life's chemical reactions. Reactions that might otherwise take many years occur in a fraction of a second with the help of enzymes.

Enzymes are catalysts, meaning they are not consumed in the reactions they accelerate, so they can be recycled and reused in successive reactions. An enzyme can process millions of substrate molecules per second. It acts by playing with chemistry, that is, by lowering the activation energy required to convert reagents into products. *Activation energy* refers to the amount of energy required to break bonds in the reagent molecules to create new bonds in product molecules.

It bears repeating: Life on Earth could not wait for enzymes to eventually show up. No enzymes, no fast reactions, no life. Most of the bio-

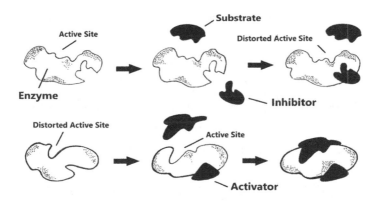

Figure 4.2. The intricate action of an enzyme accelerates chemical reactions. The target molecule is captured and properly encapsulated within the enzyme's active site. Target bonds are then formed or broken. Enzyme activity must be precisely controlled to produce life-friendly results, and happily, life has a series of enzyme activators and inhibitors to do the job.

chemical reactions required for life are intrinsically slow—lethally slow, in fact. It is logical, then, to assume they had to be anticipated and accelerated by enzymes *before* life could get going.

Many enzymes are composed of a single protein chain, which can be very sophisticated and often are enormous molecules. Conjugated enzymes are another common class of enzyme. These consist of a protein portion known as apoenzyme, inorganic cofactors such as iron, magnesium, or zinc ions, and/or organic cofactors such as vitamins or their derivatives. Such conjugated enzymes further enhance the sophistication of the system, given the greater diversity of functions and structures. Still other enzymes are composed of multiple subunits—each an individual protein that contributes to the enzyme's functioning. Sometimes the subunits carry out multiple reaction steps and hand off the intermediates from one reaction site to the next very rapidly, like hot potatoes, so the intermediates don't degrade before the next step can take place.

Enzymes are very effective, but they only work well if the medium's temperature, pH balance, and substrate concentration have been properly adjusted. Under too low or too high temperatures and pHs, an enzyme denatures—that is, loses its functional 3-D shape. Numerous life-essential enzymes require strictly controlled chemical environments, and only function properly within fully formed and functional cells. These intracellular enzymes pose another chicken-egg problem: No cell, no enzymes; no enzymes, no cell.

See the quandary? Enzymes, themselves exquisite works of engineering sophistication, need fully formed and functioning cells to survive; and cells need fully operational enzymes to survive. So you have to have both at the beginning. You can't have one pop into existence by some miracle of happenstance, and then some time later have the other pop into existence by a similar stroke of good fortune, and expect the other to still be waiting around. The first would be long dead before the second arrived, and with the first one dead, the second is in for a very short ride in Darwin's warm little pond.

Enzymes also have spectacular internal dynamics, dynamics dictated by a finely tuned intramolecular ballet. This synchronized ballet involves the movement of protein parts—everything from very small things like individual amino acids, or groups of amino acids, to a loop of the protein chain, or segments of the protein chain with particular 3-D shapes called α-helices and β-sheets (Figure 4.1), all the way up to entire protein domains. These movements are driven by finely tuned intramolecular forces and occur in as little as a few quadrillionths of a second. (A quadrillion is 1 followed by 15 zeroes—that is, a thousand trillion.) Enzymes not only position their substrates correctly in 3-D space, making it possible for them to react, but also stir them up using precise vibrations to bring about the proper conformations.

A few examples of enzymes will reveal how important they are to life. RNA polymerase, for instance, helps transcribe DNA into RNA. Aminoacyl-tRNA synthetases fit the proper amino acid to the proper tRNA, allowing the ribosomes to work properly. No enzymes, no life. And no life, no enzymes.

If one were assigned to design an effective enzyme from scratch, imagine how much prior knowledge would be needed. You would have to understand the final goal and be aware in advance of the 3-D shape of your substrate before you could create a proper cavity in the enzyme where the substrate fits (Figure 4.2). You would need to know the functional groups in the substrate that the enzyme needs to immobilize in its active site (using effective inter- and intra-molecular interactions such as hydrogen and polar bonding). You also would need to know what reaction was needed and where this reaction should occur to activate the proper site of the immobilized molecule. Finally, you would have to know how to protect your enzyme from harmful reactions with the substrate.

And all that is only the initial preparation. After that, you would need to know how to place nanomolecular "hands" in your enzyme to promote, for example, the hydrolysis of your substrate by reaction with a hand-delivered water molecule.

It is extremely hard just to describe this process, to say nothing of actually designing a system to accomplish it. Yet enzymes do it automatically, over and over again, with right-on-time delivery.

There is a lab that has begun this process of trying to make designer enzymes—David Baker's lab at the University of Washington. They choose a kind of reaction they want to create, then look for the kind of chemistry they would need to create, then find an enzyme that has an active site that comes closest to what they need. Then interactive modeling of changes to enzyme sequence and structure are run in the computer until they are satisfied they have found a sequence that comes closest to one that will work. Then they synthesize and test the enzyme. Lather, rinse, repeat multiple times. They have succeeded in creating designer enzymes but, the last time I looked, with low specific activity. Not normal yet.

The scientists and the media are excited about the possibilities of bringing intelligence to bear on the problem of enzyme design. Working from the assumption that enzymes are the product of evolutionary processes, Baker says, "There's a lot of things that nature has come up with just by randomly bumbling around." And he adds, "As we understand more and more of the basic principles, we ought to be able to do far better."[4] We'll see. It's an interesting reverse test of intelligent design, don't you think?[5]

Chaperones and Chaperonins

PROTEINS ARE marvelous pieces of chemical nanoengineering, but for these biomolecular giants to become functional, the linear strings of alpha-L-amino acids need to take on specific 3-D forms. As the protein takes shape, it folds itself thanks to numerous well-balanced intramolecular forces. But there are many possible 3-D forms, and proteins can get lost along the way. The final functional shape is its lowest free energy conformational state, but this is sometimes hard to find. If it folds into the wrong shape, a protein is useless. If the first proteins fell into these death valleys, life on Earth would never have appeared. So, what was the solution? The amazing chaperones (Figure 4.3). Here is how their role is described in the journal *Nature*:

> Most proteins must fold into defined three-dimensional structures to gain functional activity. But in the cellular environment, newly synthesized proteins are at great risk of aberrant folding and aggregation, potentially forming toxic species. To avoid these dangers, cells invest in a complex network of molecular chaperones, which use ingenious mechanisms to prevent aggregation and promote efficient folding. Because protein molecules are highly dynamic, constant chaperone surveillance is required to ensure protein homeostasis (proteostasis).[6]

Chaperones that help proteins fold into the right shape are called "chaperonins," but as we shall see below, chaperones perform other functions as well. As the authors of another study put it, "At the most elementary level, biomolecular interactions define life, and protein chaperones are designed to moderate such interactions."[7]

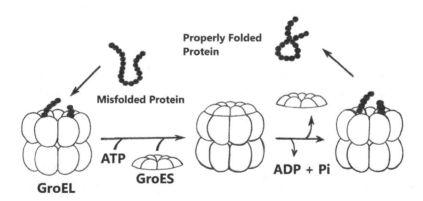

Figure 4.3. Chaperones, including chaperonins, are the "physiotherapists of life," helping "baby proteins" to get in shape. Which came first: proteins that need chaperones to fold properly, or chaperones that help to rapidly and properly fold proteins?

Spontaneous folding is quite rapid (milliseconds to seconds) for many proteins, but many large, critical proteins fail to find by themselves the right shape and, without help, would become only so much molecular waste. Also, when forming a protein complex, a protein will remain in an incorrect shape if it fails to find a partner subunit. A lot has to go right for the protein to assume its functional 3-D shape.

Properly folded proteins are essential for life because they conduct most of the necessary functions in a cell. Different kinds of chaperones exist for helping fold different kinds of proteins. One example is the chaperone HSP70, which biochemist Laurence Moran describes as binding "to hydrophobic regions of the folding protein, preventing it from aggregating with other partially folded proteins and steering it toward the final structure."[8]

Simply put, chaperones avert folding mishaps and are therefore crucial in protein synthesis. The way protein folding is controlled varies from protein to protein. Some chaperones help fold certain amino acid chains while they are still being constructed by the ribosomes. Post-translation chaperones do this job after translation is completed for other proteins. One chaperone, Trigger Factor, slows down improper folding of amino acid chains, and can even unfold amino acid chains that have already folded incorrectly.

Many proteins require chaperones to fold rapidly and properly. Instead of spontaneous self-assembly we find assisted assembly. And even after the proteins are folded correctly, chaperones help them maintain their functional states, by a process known as proteostasis.[9]

Such work is indispensable. Misfolded proteins are not merely useless to the cell, but ruinous. Their exposed hydrophobic surfaces bind to each other, causing misfolded proteins to start clumping together. In some inherited human diseases, these clumps of misfolded proteins can cause severe symptoms and even death. Chaperones are normally able to prevent such protein clumping by binding to the exposed hydrophobic surfaces using hydrophobic surfaces of their own. Usually, incorrectly folded proteins have exposed patches of hydrophobic amino acids on their surfaces, while correctly folded proteins usually have these hydrophobic amino acids buried in their interior.

These protein rescuers compete with another mechanism for clean-up duty. This second mechanism, upon recognizing an abnormally exposed hydrophobic patch in the structure of a protein, marks the protein for destruction by large aggregates of protein-eating enzymes called "proteasomes." The normal functioning of chaperones and proteasomes masterfully prevents runaway protein clumping in a cell.

And here's the kicker. For cells to function, chaperones are essential to fold and maintain the cell's crucial proteins.[10] In addition to helping fold, chaperones also assist under conditions of cellular stress. For instance, what are known as *heat shock proteins* (HSPs) chaperone back to their original shape other proteins that have been damaged by thermal shock. Without them, no life. And yet chaperones are themselves made of proteins that must be properly folded and maintained by other kinds of chaperones.[11] For those committed to origin-of-life scenarios devoid of foresight and planning, this is a devilishly difficult chicken-egg problem.

The aforementioned Laurence Moran, a professor of biochemistry at the University of Toronto, disagrees:

> All of the common chaperones fold spontaneously without the assistance of any other chaperones. The reason why they are called "heat shock" proteins is because their synthesis is induced when cells encounter high temperature or other conditions that may cause proteins to unfold or become unstable. These rescue chaperones are made in huge quantities under these conditions to help prevent the destruction of normal cellular proteins. If you understand this then you will understand that the chaperones themselves are capable of rapid spontaneous folding.[12]

Contrast Moran's picture of chaperones quickly and easily "folding without the assistance of any other chaperones" with a comment on the matter by Per Hammarström, a professor in the Department of Physics, Chemistry, and Biology at Linköping University, Sweden. Hammarström is co-author of an article on chaperone folding published in the *Journal of Chemical Biology*. This paper deals with two chaperone proteins called GroES and GroEL, both heat shock proteins that are activated in response to stress, and that work together to assist in folding or refolding proteins. They have been shown to interact with up to 30% of the cell's proteins, so their importance is real. Together they form a barrel-shaped structure, with GroEL the main part of the barrel and GroES the lid. Unfolded proteins enter the barrel and after several cycles of binding and release, are let go into the cytoplasm again, now folded.

In responding to a question posted at Research Gate about chaperone folding, Hammarström noted that "we have very recently shown that GroES the co-chaperone is likely assisting in folding GroEL." This comment, combined with previous work published in *Nature*[13], suggests that chaperones do indeed serve as chaperones to other chaperones—GroES helps to fold GroEL. In addition, the *Journal of Chemical Biology* paper says that "translation and thus protein synthesis of GroES and GroEL are spatially organized according to gene order. Therefore, GroES will first be synthesized facilitating its interaction with the subsequently formed GroEL. It is hence intriguing to propose that GroEL is a substrate for GroES."[14] That is, GroEL is acted upon by GroES.

In sum, an existing GroES may be needed to help fold a newly forming GroEL; whereupon they both work in synchrony to help fold other key proteins.

The Shocking Skill of Heat Shock Proteins

BRUCE ALBERTS and his colleagues note that these heat-shock proteins "are synthesized in dramatically increased amounts after a brief exposure of cells to an elevated temperature." For instance, the optimal temperature for human cells is 98.6°F, but if they are exposed to a temperature 8 or 9 degrees above that, they will experience heat shock. This reflects the operation of a feedback system that "responds to an increase in misfolded proteins... by boosting the synthesis of the chaperones that help these proteins refold."[15]

As F. Ulrich Hartl and his colleagues explain, HSP70 chaperones "are multicomponent molecular machines that promote folding through ATP- and cofactor-regulated binding and release cycles." HSP70 is itself regulated by nucleotide-exchange factor proteins and by proteins from the HSP40 family.[16] Proteins that still fail to fold properly with the help of these chaperones are then treated by the toughest physiotherapists of life: the *chaperonins*, large, cage-like, "double-ring complexes... that function by globally enclosing substrate proteins... for folding." Chaperonins function as a kind of backstop. "The cylindrical chaperonins allow the folding of single protein molecules enclosed in a cage," Hartl et al. write. "The two systems act sequentially, whereby HSP70 interacts upstream with nascent and newly synthesized polypeptides and the chaperonins function downstream in the final folding of those proteins that fail to reach native state by cycling on HSP70 alone."[17]

To the benefit of science, we should then ask: Could this incredible and highly diversified system of error recognition and correction, involving a myriad of highly selective and sophisticated macromolecules, arise by an unguided and blind natural process? Darwinists have answered with a loud "yes" to this question and "explained" the emergence of chaperones by relying on vague just-so stories. But these stories are starved of specifics on how these wonders of nanotechnology could have evolved one plausible mutational step at a time.

Consider, for example, the following proposal by Moran, who wrote an essay on chaperones entitled "Protein Folding, Chaperones, and IDiots." (The last word in the title is a slur aimed at advocates of intelligent design.)

> In the beginning, you didn't need chaperones because every protein folded rapidly on its own. Some of these primitive proteins might have been a bit slow to fold so the evolution of the first chaperones was advantageous because it enhanced the rate of folding for these proteins.

The chaperones weren't absolutely necessary for survival but they conferred a selective advantage on those cells that had them.

Once chaperones were present, new proteins could evolve that would otherwise have been too slow to fold in the absence of chaperones. Over time, cells accumulated more and more of these slowly folding proteins so that today no cell can survive without chaperones.[18]

Moran's explanation for chaperones slips into obvious biochemical errors. Many essential functions of life, functions that all life forms have, require chaperone-assisted folding proteins. Recent findings have only broadened the essential roles of chaperone biology. "There have been a number of recent discoveries," R. A. Quinlan and R. J. Ellis report, "that extend this relatively neglected aspect of chaperone biology to include proteostasis, maintenance of the cellular redox potential, genome stability, transcriptional regulation, and cytoskeletal dynamics."[19] These processes are central to life. As Quinlan and Ellis put it, "Chaperones stand at the crossroads of life and death because they mediate essential functions, not only during the bad times, but also in the good times."[20]

The odds are therefore vanishingly small that life could have existed with only self-folding proteins. These proteins would have been too few, and life has been found to require hundreds of proteins expressed by at least 250 essential genes—1,000 or more if we realistically consider a fully independent form of life.[21] The probability of hundreds of essential proteins all folding into the correct shape at proper speed on their own without mistakes beggars rational belief. Toxic clumps of useless, misfolded proteins are astronomically easier to form than functional ones.

Further, even if functional proteins could form by some stroke of extraordinary good luck, it would take too long, and the various protein types needed for a viable single-celled life form would have no meaningful chance of finding each other in the same place and thus able to assemble into a functioning whole. Each of the miracle proteins would die a quick, lonely death before it found the other proteins. Without chaperones, no viable cells.

Moran's explanation is an instance of what I refer to as the "why-with-no-how" evolutionary fallacy. It's easy to explain the advantage ("why") of a feature; the "how," with the corresponding mechanisms and detailed evolutionary pathway at the molecular level, is largely or wholly ignored. Such "explanations" fail to consider the immense risk and difficulties of such an evolutionary leap. For Moran, the appearance of chaperones is justified simply by the advantage it would confer. But by offering no reasonable evolutionary pathway, he fails to explain *how*, biochemically, such a feature could have evolved.

Flagellar Filament Caps

LIFE IS full of problems that must be solved, and the way they are solved is amazing. There are so many molecular marvels that should give us pause. Take for example a problem that the lowly bacterium must solve—getting to its next meal. For the bacterium *E. coli*, and many other bacteria, the solution has been to build flagella.

The bacterial flagellum motor (Figure 4.4) was brought to popular attention by biochemist Michael Behe, who presented this spectacular nanomachine as a challenge to the modern theory of evolution. Whatever your views on that interpretation, one thing is beyond controversy: The bacterial flagellum is a nanoengineering wonder of the first rank.

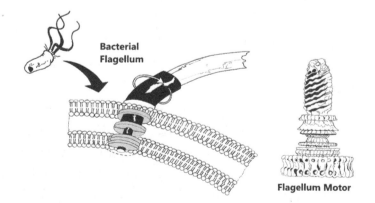

Figure 4.4. Details of the flagellum motor, arguably the most spectacular engine on Earth.

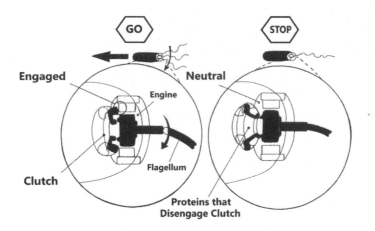

Figure 4.5. The amazing clutch system on the flagellum motor.

The flagellum motor is composed of forty to fifty protein complexes, which require millions of atoms in each. All these many millions of atoms are perfectly arranged to make the flagellum motor and tail. Thousands upon thousands of ingeniously and sequentially arranged amino acids in the alpha-L amino acid chains of these proteins experience perfect nanometric equilibria of inter- and intramolecular forces to fold properly and fit together in a synchronized fashion. These nanomolecular pieces, with perfect 3-D structures, function and look like rotors, shafts, stators, O-rings, junctions, a propeller, and even a clutch.

We have heard elsewhere about the intricacies of the motor's parts and function; there is also more to the story about the genetic control of its assembly than we have time to tell here. However, one detail of the flagellar structure stands out: the perfect intertwining of four protein wires that make up its filament (Figure 4.6). The flagellar filament, which acts as a propeller, may be ten times longer than the cell itself. It is a well-ordered, long, helical screw-like assembly with a hollow tube about twenty nanometers in diameter. It is made of a flagellin protein arranged in individual helical threads, which wrap around one another, like the threads in a rope, to form a braid.

Overall, this filament displays a relatively inflexible helical shape, like a stretched-out corkscrew that propels the bacterium straight forward when it rotates. As Koji Yonekura, Saori Maki-Yonekura, and Keiichi Namba note, the tubular structures comprise "eleven protofilaments, which are nearly longitudinal helical arrays of subunits."[22] And that just scratches the surface of the sophistication involved. How was such a thing ever assembled in the first place?

Setting aside the question of its origin in the past, it's daunting enough to understand how this marvelous swimming machine assembles itself here in the present. Wire strands left on their own become a tangled mess, like earbuds at the bottom of a backpack. To prevent this mess, the flagellum has a 3-D cap, a spectacular nanomolecular template (Figure 4.6). This perfectly-molded nanomolecular guide, with "its pentagon-shaped plate and its carefully crafted leg-like extensions," as one writer described it, functions "as a rotary promoter for self-assembly of flagellin monomers,"[23] perfectly guiding the synchronized sliding of the wires through it.

This capping protein, when at work, sits atop the hollow flagellar filament and guides assembly using five leg domains, which point down and fit into cavities situated at the distal tip of the emerging filament.[24] This interlacing makes the final tail strong, resistant, and perfect. But

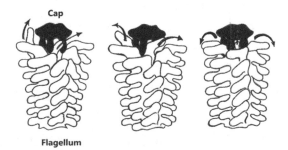

Figure 4.6. The intricate and carefully designed cap that guides the long, helical screw-like assembly of flagellin protein wires, making them wrap around one another to form the braid-like flagellar filament.

how does this perfect wire grow? At the base of the flagellum, a type III secretory system pumps flagellin monomers (the nanomolecular wires) through the interior of the tail, in formation. Each flagellum strand already installed pushes the new wire into the protein molecular mold, twisting it to perfection as the tail grows.

Many bacteria must move to find food. For them, a flagellum is necessary for survival. Developing a flagellum is no small matter. In *Darwin's Black Box*, Michael Behe argued that it could not have evolved one random mutation at a time because there is no viable evolutionary pathway. The thing, as he put it, is irreducibly complex. Evolutionists have argued[25] that the irreducibly complex flagellum motor could have arisen stepwise, and they have invoked various non-design, Darwinian explanations, but their proposed scenarios are universally starved of detail.

But the capping protein may be the bigger challenge for those committed to blind evolution, since it only seems to serve a single purpose within the cell and is useless without the flagellin monomers it helps assemble. And without such a cap to guide assembly, the flagellin monomers are of no use either.[26] So which evolved first?

The most famous of the evolutionary proposals is the cooption model, which assumes the use of parts already available from other systems, such as the type III secretory system. Biologist Kenneth Miller writes, "The point, which science has long understood, is that bits and pieces of supposedly irreducibly complex machines may have different—but still useful—functions... Evolution produces complex biochemical machines by copying, modifying, and combining proteins previously used for other functions."[27]

But this "explanation" contains zero chemistry with a heaping dose of rhetoric and morphological analogies. Miller's cooption argument is flawed because the whole flagellum (especially a piece such as the cap) requires foresight. The only way to save such an argument would be to count on the help of some kind of Darwinian MacGyver to perform the insane nanomolecular super-tasks of "copying, modifying, and combining" all the molecular parts, and doing so with the extreme precision the flagellum demands.

Although Miller's argument gained some traction early on, it is now recognized that, even on the assumption that modern evolutionary theory is true, type III secretory systems are recent innovations, probably derived from more complex flagella, and not flagellar progenitors. With regard to the evolution of the flagellum, one of its leading investigators, Shin-Ichi Aizawa, is worth quoting. "Since the flagellum is so well designed and beautifully constructed by an ordered assembly pathway, even I, who am not a creationist, get an awe-inspiring feeling from its 'divine' beauty," Aizawa writes. "However, if the flagellum has evolved from a primitive form, where are the remnants of its ancestor? Why don't we see any simpler forms of flagella than what they are today? How was it possible that the flagella have evolved without leaving traces in history?"[28]

Molecular machines have always fascinated me. And the more I study them, the more amazed I am at the intricate solutions these tiny mechanisms represent. The more, too, I am convinced that such solutions show that crucial problems were recognized ahead of time and solved. This act of anticipation—foresight—is not a characteristic of blind material processes. It is an act of intelligence, of a mind.

5. Bacteria, Bugs, and Carnivorous Plants

So far, we have looked at examples of foresight in the tiniest life forms on Earth: cells and the unimaginably small molecular machines that keep them running. But beautiful examples of planning are not limited to cells. They exist in all forms of life, from the smallest to the largest. In this chapter, we will look at how some of Earth's smallest creatures, and some of its more unusual plants, have features that anticipate problems and solve them in many ingenious ways.

Microbes: Another Chicken-and-Egg Paradox

Planet Earth is magnificently equipped to host life. But the phenomenon of life itself creates life-threatening problems. For example, the nitrogen molecule N_2, or $N \equiv N$, is the perfect "inert" gas for our atmosphere. But we also need nitrogen available in a more reactive form, atomic Nitrogen (N), to make amino acids (general formula $RCHNH_2COOH$) and proteins. So how can $N \equiv N$, a very stable molecule connected by a triple bond, be converted into atomic N? How can it be preserved in useful chemical forms? And how can N_2 be replenished? The supply of N_2 would eventually run out as living things constantly consumed it. A way of restoring N_2 was therefore needed.

The solution? Microbes.

Microbes are co-inhabitants on our planet and play a crucial role in maintaining life on Earth. In the oceans, plankton maintain the carbon cycle and single-celled algae called diatoms provide a fifth of our atmosphere's oxygen (O_2). On land and in the oceans, microbes break apart N_2 and fix it into such compounds as ammonia (NH_3).[1] Other bacteria take NH_3 and convert it back to N_2 in what is called the nitrogen cycle. The tiniest creatures on Earth maintain its habitability for all of us.

Free oxygen (O_2) and carbon (C) are also essential for the habitability of Earth, and they too have refreshment cycles that rely on microbes as well as plants. Much of the free O_2 on Earth is produced by photosynthesis in autotrophic microbes. (Autotrophs make energy-containing organic molecules from inorganic molecules; heterotrophs make use of food that comes from other organisms.) Autotrophic microbes have the know-how to "fix" nitrogen by dismantling the triple bonds of atmospheric N_2 into NH_3 and other useful compounds. These microbial workhorses also maintain the balance of many other essential atmospheric elements. Without that balance, complex life could not exist. No microbes, no other life.

Anammox and Its Rocket Chemistry

BACTERIA ARE often seen as rudimentary forms of life. But one look at their molecular structure is enough to convince us otherwise. Bacteria are extremely sophisticated, fully equipped with many exquisite molecular machines.

One very strange group of bacteria discovered in the early 1990s, called anammox,[2] provides a great example of the high-tech characteristics of bacteria. According to Laura van Niftrik and Mike Jetten, anammox bacteria are found in a wide variety of environments, including low-oxygen marine zones, treatment plant wastewater, coastal sediments, and lakes.[3] It turns out that these bacteria are crucial to life on Earth: It is estimated they contribute up to fifty percent of N_2 production from marine environments,[4] resulting in the removal of fixed nitrogen.

When discovered, anammox bacteria caused a real scientific stir. They are major players in Earth's biogeochemical nitrogen cycle, and scientists wondered how such simple bacteria could perform a reaction previously considered impossible.[5] Anammox converts NH_3 and NO_2^- into N_2 under anaerobic conditions, that is, in the absence of O_2.

That is where it got its name: ANaerobic AMMonium OXidation.[6] Van Niftrick and Jetten note that "Anammox bacteria do not conform to the typical characteristics of bacteria but instead share features with all three domains of life, Bacteria, Archaea, and Eukarya, making them extremely interesting from an evolutionary perspective."[7] I would go further and say that the existence of these crucial and unusual bacteria is in fact extremely difficult to explain from an evolutionary perspective.

How does an anammox bacterium fulfill its indispensable mission of replenishing nitrogen? It uses rocket science and some highly sophisticated organic synthesis skills.

The bacterium has an internal organelle covered by a double-layer membrane, not at all peculiar in prokaryotic cells. The greatest surprise was what was *inside* the organelle. Inside, scientists found hydrazine, which has a variety of uses, including for rocket fuel![8] Anammox somehow makes, stores, and uses a highly toxic, corrosive, and explosive liquid.

Can you imagine a creature evolving one step at a time to store this stuff inside itself? Imagine trying to synthesize pure hydrazine by trial and error inside a bacterium. It wouldn't take long to kill it! How would a bacterium evolve a hydrazine synthesis protocol without all the machinery to safely hold and use hydrazine? Is it plausible that a bacterium gained the ability to use pure, toxic, and explosive hydrazine by a step-by-step process that has no way to predict the future advantages of the poison? Why would a proto-anammox bacterium, which had previously not used hydrazine, and survived just fine without it, risk its life to evolve the ability to produce and store hydrazine, before it would do it any good?

Another surprise is that anammox bacteria store hydrazine in internal compartments called anammoxosomes.[9] Obviously, anammox bacteria must handle this explosive molecule with the greatest care. Chemical and microscopic analysis of the anammoxosome double-layer membrane, which encloses the hydrazine, revealed another surprise: The membrane consists of unique and bizarre lipids made from "ladderanes."[10] These are highly sophisticated chemical structures that many synthetic chemists would not even attempt to make.

A typical ladderane is pentacycloanammoxic acid, which is composed of five fused rings of cyclobutane. It resembles a ladder and contains concatenated square ring structures formed by fused four-carbon rings. Concatenated four-membered rings are one of the hardest to make because kinetics and thermodynamics work against them. But anammox bacteria seem to have skipped organic synthesis classes and gone ahead and built them anyway.

But why go to all the effort? It appears that anammox bacteria did it only to use hydrazine as an agent to convert NH_3 and NO_2^- into N_2 in the absence of O_2. So why would a bacterium synthesize N_2, an almost inert gas that is practically useless for life as such? Anammox bacteria live all over the world. They are abundant in the oceans. They undertake this nearly impossible task simply to produce N_2. But because of this "charity effort," they regulate the N_2 cycle and maintain the O_2/N_2 ratio of the Earth's atmosphere.[11] This little nanomolecular machine keeps the N_2 at the balance needed for all life forms on our planet to survive. In essence, this little microbe uses rocket science[12] to make life on earth possible, and sustainable.

And we're only beginning to understand this extraordinary bacterium. The enzymatic mechanism that makes hydrazine must also be incredible. As described by Andreas Dietl and his colleagues, "The crystal structure implies a two-step mechanism for hydrazine synthesis: a three-electron reduction of nitric oxide to hydroxylamine at the active site of the γ-subunit and its subsequent condensation with ammonia." The authors of the *Nature* paper go on to note a striking parallel: "Interestingly, the proposed scheme is analogous to the Raschig process used in industrial hydrazine synthesis."[13]

So, again we find that another of our carefully planned inventions is only following in nature's footsteps. The N_2 gas that pairs with O_2 in our atmosphere and is essential for life on Earth is, as another article puts it, "a byproduct of an exquisitely designed, precision nanomachine that knows a lot about organic redox chemistry and safe handling of rocket fuel."[14]

The world of microbes proves more sophisticated with every discovery, manifesting more and more "surprises"—that is, evidence of foresight. Recently, we discovered another microbial wonder: the enigmatic comammox,[15] or "complete ammonia oxidizer." This bacterium can be found almost everywhere and does an even more spectacular job than anammox. Comammox perform complete nitrification on their own, a milestone of microbiology. Two different classes of nitrifier microbes have long been known to cooperate in carrying out the nitrification process where NH_3 is oxidized to NO_2^-, which is subsequently oxidized to NO_3^-. But the comammox doesn't share labor in nitrification. It catalyzes both nitrification steps, doing complete ammonia oxidation and thus conserving energy.

It is difficult to escape the implications of all this: The need to sustain an atmosphere suited to life had to be anticipated from the start. And an array of microbes, equipped with a sophisticated arsenal of chemicals and capacities, had to be provided to meet that need.

Issus: The Inventor of Gears?

FOR FLIGHTLESS insects, the ability to jump high, fast, and with great precision is essential for their survival. To avoid being eaten, a flightless insect must be able to jump from the time it is born. It should come as no surprise, therefore, that small insects are among the best jumpers on this planet.

But light insects with small bodies taking large leaps pose a big engineering problem. To make matters more difficult, insects have pairs of legs, so the leaping action must be perfectly coordinated, the legs pushing forward more or less simultaneously. There's not much room for trial and error.

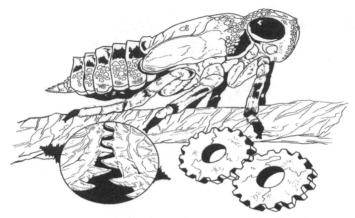

Figure 5.1. Nymphalid planthoppers, flea-sized insects in the genus *Issus*, use exquisitely engineered gears to synchronize the catapult-like movement of their legs for precision jumping.

How do these creatures manage it? What follows is one particularly extraordinary strategy.

In 2013, two biologists at the University of Cambridge, Malcolm Burrows and Gregory Sutton, were studying a tiny insect, a nymphalid planthopper in the genus *Issus* (Figure 5.1), a creature found throughout Europe and North Africa. What they discovered sounds like something off the pages of *Popular Mechanics'* What's New section. This tiny insect jumps using *interlocking gears* on its hindleg trochanters, which connect the legs to the insect equivalent of a hip.[16]

Using this miniaturized technology, these tiny insects, barely larger than a flea, move their legs in near-perfect coordination. Because both legs swing laterally, if one were extended a split second before the other, the insect would end up in a spin and become easy food. But the gears are so finely engineered that the creatures can jump fast, far, and straight.

Their cuticular mechanical gears intermesh and rotate with great precision, coordinating the legs. Each gear rotates within thirty millionths of a second of the other at more than 33,000 RPM (revolutions per minute). The highest-revving production sports car engines only reach around 10,000 RPM.

The gears also synchronously cock the legs before triggering forward jumps, using asymmetric (better than symmetric) teeth. Burrows and Sutton explained that "close registration between the gears ensured that both hindlegs moved at the same angular velocities to propel the insect's body without yaw rotation (twisting about a vertical axis).[17] Infant *Issus* can jump one hundred times their length and at speeds as high as 3.9 meters per second.

But the risk of breaking such a tiny high-speed device is high. To offset this risk, the gears are constantly replaced by new ones in the juvenile insect. As Burrows and Sutton suggested, the juvenile *Issus* repeatedly develop new gears as they grow so that if the gear is damaged, they just have to survive for a short period until a new, undamaged pair has arrived.

For the heavier adult, the gears are changed out for a more robust device suitable to the adult's larger size—a high-performance friction-based mechanism. This too suggests foresight.

At present it appears that the juvenile nymphalid planthopper *Issus* is the only creature that uses interlocking toothed mechanical gears to perfectly synchronize its limbs for long-distance jumps. Until this discovery, gears had never before been found to allow ballistic jumping movements. If evolution somehow created this engineering marvel, it seems to have done it as a one-off.

In discussing the most likely origin for the *Issus* gears, Sutton correctly considered the two scientifically possible options, but then selected the wrong one—the one that lacks the demonstrated capacity for engineering such marvels. He wrote, "These gears are not designed; they are evolved—representing high speed and precision machinery evolved for synchronization in the animal world."[18] As is usual with such claims, it is not followed by an account of how this gear-based jumping system might have evolved one small functional step at a time, a pathway essential if some form of blind Darwinian evolution produced it. But no matter; we apparently are expected to embrace that scenario as settled dogma anyway.

Instead, let's reason through the claim. Suppose, for the sake of argument, that *Issus* had existed and was able to live long enough to escape extinction without the juvenile gear or an adult friction mechanism. Why would it risk evolving two new, distinct jumping mechanisms? Because evolution works in small steps, it must make an imperfect gear or friction system first. Suppose it switched things and gave the gears to the adult and the friction mechanism to the juvenile? The poor mutant *Issus* would test out this new function, only to find out it failed to work.

And even if evolution selected the right age for each function, infant *Issus* would discover that the new gear material was too soft, or the number and spacing of the teeth were off, or the push was too much to the right or to the left, causing the creature to spin out of control and crash. There are numerous things that could go wrong. An imperfect gear system, in this case, is no good at all.

And which came first? Gears for the juvenile, or the friction system better suited for the adult *Issus*? It would need both, since the creature would always need to be able to jump to survive, as a juvenile and as an adult. Plan and deliver an exquisitely engineered pair of jumping systems from the start—one for the juvenile and one for the adult—or *adios*, little insect.

Unquestionably, the *Issus* gears are an example of high technology. One final piece of evidence to drive home the point: The risk for such high-tech and demanding 33,000+ RPM gears is great: If any tooth is damaged, the effectiveness of the designed gear is lost. To minimize the risk, the eighty-millionths-of-a-meter-wide teeth are equipped with filleted curves at the base. Humans eventually invented similar techniques to get more torque and reduce wear over time, but nature got there first.

Functional gears of any kind are ingeniously crafted devices. They come in many forms and are used for many purposes. They are a keystone of modern technology, present in many types of machinery, cars, and bicycles. As far as human history goes, it seems that no one knows for sure who invented mechanical gears, but we do know the Greeks used them in the world's earliest known analogical computer, the Antikythera mechanism, which is now thought to have been used to chart the movements of the sun, the moon, and the planets visible to the naked eye.[19] When in 1900 Greek sponge divers found this ancient mechanism—the most advanced technological mechanism as yet discovered from antiquity—and they saw the gears, they immediately recognized it as the product of an intelligent mind. If no other type of cause has the demonstrated capacity to generate such marvels, why should we respond differently when we find exquisitely crafted gears attached to the legs of a jumping insect, particularly when the imaginative stories of the blind evolution of such natural wonders go begging for credible detail?

Tyson Packs a Punch

IN 1998, Tyson astonished the world by smashing a hole in the wall imprisoning him in England, using just his bare hands.[20] Tyson was soon all over the news. But no, we're not talking about heavy-weight boxer Mike Tyson. This Tyson is a tiny ocean creature that smashed the quarter-inch-thick glass of its tank at England's Great Yarmouth Sea Life Centre. Pound for pound, this Tyson is unbeatable when it comes to throwing the fastest and most powerful punches.

Tyson was a peacock mantis shrimp (*Odontodactylus scyllarus*). This species uses appendages modified into clubs to generate an extremely fast strike to smash shells.[21] Such powerful punches require both energy storage and a release system, in the form of a saddle-shaped exoskeletal spring mechanism.

Scientists have studied the strikes using high-speed imaging equipment. They found that Mantis shrimp deliver one of the fastest underwater punches on Earth, reaching a top speed of fifty miles per hour in less than 800 microseconds, and generating a force reaching close to 2,500 times the animal's body weight.[22] The strikes are so fast and so powerful that they produce small flashes of light by lowering the surrounding water pressure so much that it boils. Small bubbles collapse when the water pressure normalizes, unleashing an enormous quantity of energy by cavitation. "The club reaches its target in just three thousandths of a second," writes Ed Yong, "and strikes with the force of a rifle bullet."[23] And it manages this not in the air but underwater, that is, while working against the substantial drag imposed by water.

It's an elegant, state-of-the-art technology. As Dr. Sheila Patek, co-author of a paper[24] on the shrimp, told *BBC*, "Much like an archer, the mantis shrimp stores up elastic energy in advance of the strike and releases it with a latch."[25] (Figure 5.2)

Yong elaborates. "Once the arm is cocked, a ratchet locks it firmly in place," he writes. "The large muscles in the upper arm then contract and build up energy. When the latch is released, all this energy is released at once and the lower arm is launched forwards."[26]

Patek, T. I. Zack, and T. Claverie further note, "The remarkable shapes and mineralization patterns that characterize the mantis shrimp's

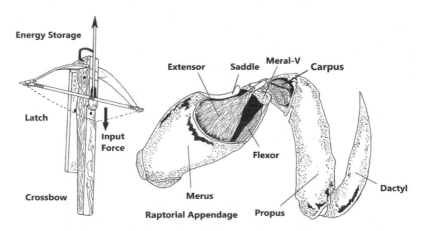

Figure 5.2. The mantis shrimp's club-like appendage system works like a crossbow, delivering one of the most powerful punches on Earth. In proportion to its body size, it beats former heavyweight champion boxer Mike Tyson by an order of magnitude.

raptorial appendage further reveal a highly integrated mechanical power amplification system based on exoskeletal elastic energy storage."[27]

A key feature of this powerful jab is is a tiny structure in the arm that is reminiscent of a saddle, which is also compressed during cocking and functions like a spring, storing additional energy. When the latch releases, the saddle-like structure expands and provides additional push for the club, accelerating it at upwards of 10,000 g-forces,[28] powerful enough to shatter the glass of a shrimp tank. The design is similar to one used by human engineers.

But how can the mantis shrimp deliver punches so quickly and powerfully without injuring itself? The shrimp comes equipped with its own high-tech boxing glove.

We have only recently uncovered this engineering marvel.[29] The frontal impact region of the club is very thick and made of a bone-like material: hydroxyapatite crystals. Angled perpendicularly to the surface, each crystal forms a column that provides high compressive strength and can take up to four billion pascals of pressure. (Air pressure at sea level is about 100,000 pascals.) How does that structure compare to human technology? Forged at extremely high temperatures of over 2,700°F, human-made analogues such as ceramics can take only two or three billion pascals of pressure.

Next to the impact region are protein fibers ingeniously designed in stacked layers. "In each one, the fibers are all parallel, but each layer is rotated slightly from the one underneath it to produce a helical structure," Yong writes. "Finally, the space between the fibers is filled with haphazardly arranged minerals," preventing any cracks from spreading through the club. The mantis shrimp's club is further wrapped in chitin fibers, compressing the entire structure to slow the spread of cracks, "like a boxer who places tape around their fists," as described by Dr. David Kisalius.[30]

Evolutionary theory claims that mantis shrimp evolved all these features to fill special needs posed by their environment. *National Geographic* science writer Ed Yong explains: "Some scientists think that the mantis shrimps' belligerent nature evolved because the rock crevices they inhabit are fiercely contested. This competition has also made these animals smarter than the average shrimp. They are the only invertebrates that can recognize other individuals of their species and can remember the outcome of a fight against a rival for up to a month."[31] All that is to say, if punching hard and being smart in a tough neighborhood comes in handy, evolution will come to the rescue with power punches and an IQ boost. It's a nice story but fails to explain how the tiny shrimp actually developed all this technology and know-how by unguided trial and error, one small functional mutation at a time. All the pieces of the punching mechanism had to be in place for it to work, so it's reasonable to doubt that such an evolutionary pathway is really possible.

Carnivorous Plants

CARNIVOROUS PLANTS (Figure 5.3) are intriguing, bizarre, and hard not to love at first sight. These plants use an arsenal of masterfully engineered moving traps, chemical and electrical sensors, and digestive chemicals to kill and consume spiders, insects, protozoans, crustaceans, lizards, mice, rats, and various other small invertebrates and vertebrates. Each of these carnivorous plants manages all this using lures and a trap device, along with a mechanism and an arsenal of chemicals to facilitate full digestion of the prey.[32]

Figure 5.3. The carnivorous plant, the Venus flytrap, with its trap open, closed, and during the digestion phase.

As Aaron Ellison and Nicholas Gotelli note, Charles Darwin pioneered the modern research of carnivorous plants with his 1875 work *Insectivorous Plants*. There Darwin applied his idea of homology (which modern evolutionary biologists call "homoplasy") to highlight what he saw as evolutionary convergence across apparently unrelated taxa, and he was the first to provide descriptions of the structures that eight genera of plants use to entrap insects.[33]

As Darwin reported, these plants are impressive not only for being able to capture prey but also for employing specific enzymes to dissolve the animal proteins and then absorb them. If no enzymes were there, there would be no use for the trap at all. Although Darwin described all this nearly 150 years ago, since then no work has shown *how* these amazing creatures could have evolved their intricate and highly synchronized anatomical, electrical, and biochemical functions.

Carnivorous plants use highly specialized leaves that function as mechanical traps. "Many traps lure prey with bright colors, extra-floral nectaries, guide hairs, and/or leaf extensions," writes John Brittnacher. "Once caught and killed, the prey is digested by the plant and/or partner organisms. The plant then absorbs the nutrients made available from the corpse. Most carnivorous plants will grow without consuming prey but they grow much faster and reproduce much better with nutrients derived from their prey."[34]

The Venus flytrap, *Dionaea muscipula*, is the most famous carnivorous plant.[35] In its wild habitat in the southeastern United States, it mostly eats flies, but it will consume anything living that fits in the trap. As Rainer Hedrich and Erwin Neher explain, the plant employs highly sensitive mechanoreceptors, and "upon contact with prey an action potential is triggered which, via an electrical network—comparable to the nervous system of vertebrates—rapidly closes its bivalved trap."[36] (Figure 5.4)[37]

The trap snaps shut automatically, but then the plant follows a carefully orchestrated sequence of gene activation to tightly close the trap,

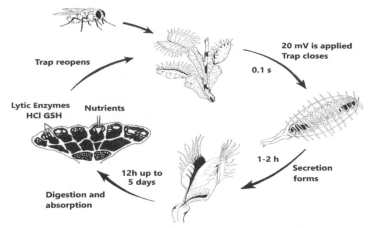

Figure 5.4. An amazing cycle of events occurs when the Venus flytrap opens its bivalved trap. It detects its prey through electrical chemosensors, captures it by quickly closing the trap, digests the prey using selective enzymes, and drinks the juice before reopening the trap.

digest the prey, and absorb the nutrients. This whole sequence of events must happen in perfect synchrony. The plant makes step-by-step decisions about activation by counting the stimuli on its sensory organs.

Evolutionary scientists have not dared to propose that the Venus flytrap evolved these animal-like skills by taking genes from its prey, a nearly impossible feat since the prey is fully digested for food. Rather, they have suggested the plant modified and rearranged gene functions that all plants share. But this too lies well beyond the reach of a blind process that cannot predict future needs.

Carnivory is found in the animal kingdom and makes the most sense there. That's why it's so intriguing to find this behavior in the green branch of the tree of life, especially considering that most plants seem to thrive using just photosynthesis. If carnivory evolved here to provide more nutrients, why would natural selection reward the plants—apparently able to benefit from more nutrients—for expending some of the precious nutrients they already had to evolve a not-yet-useful new nutrient supply tool, and reward these supposedly evolving plants for their seemingly far-sighted efforts over countless generations stretching over long ages? That is, if the nutrition from the carnivorous action was just a non-essential bonus for the flower, then why would nature select for all the many intermediate steps of this complex bonus system during which the system offered no benefit—neither nutrition nor protection—and likely exacted a nutrient and energy cost at the risk of survival?

If it first evolved for protection and then later evolved to provide additional nutrients, we have the same problem: Why expend all the energy on the way to a functional protection system, before the protection system was at all functional? Natural selection does not look ahead to future payoff, remember. It's all about "What have you done for me lately?"

This challenge for Darwinism is only exacerbated by the fact that, if indeed they did evolve carnivory, these plants had to do so "independently at least six times in five angiosperm orders," as Ellison and Gotelli explain.[38]

Maybe one could grant the evolutionary miracle a single time, but six times?

Other plants, such as *Darlingtonia* and some *Nepenthes* species, are believed to have lost the ability to digest prey themselves. Perhaps the digestive system worked fine, but then the plant found itself in an environment rich enough in bacteria and other organisms that one of these plants born with a defective, poorly functioning digestive system could manage just fine. In such situations, the plant could rely on the bacteria and other organisms now in its environment to digest the nutrients from the prey it captured.

On its website, the International Carnivorous Plant Society explains this in the following way: "To put it unscientifically, why should a plant go through all the bother of digesting the prey itself when other organisms will do it for them? Or scientifically, if there is no selective advantage to expending the energy for digestion, mutations will accumulate eliminating digestion."[39]

Maybe so, but that is devolution—breaking an existing system. And as anyone who has had children knows, any two-year-old can manage that. Darwinism needs to explain the evolution of new systems, new engineering marvels, not the devolution of existing ones.[40]

Someone might complain that one just needs a bit of imagination to embrace the possibility that such plants evolved. But truly imagining a viable evolutionary pathway means describing a series of viable steps from beginning to completed trap and digestive system. Believing something happened isn't the same as imagining how it happened. Nobody has come remotely close to doing the latter, and not for lack of trying.

Are we allowed to imagine, to consider, other possible causes—causes with the demonstrated ability to assemble novel engineering marvels? Let's go ahead and consider another possibility, whether or not we have permission: The construction of the system required foresight of what would end up inside the trap in order to synchronize construction of an appropriate digestive system. It required foresight of a functioning digestive system to bother constructing the sophisticated trap. And foresight was required to construct each of the two systems individually.

A Power Unique

IT'S EASY to write off some living things as simple and primitive. But once you zoom in, using powerful microscopes and biochemistry, you find that even minuscule aspects of life are intricate beyond imagining. The microscope opens a whole world of complex, awe-inspiring structures that ingeniously solve what would otherwise be dead-end problems. And as we move up the size scale to things like the nymphalid planthopper, the Tyson shrimp, and carnivorous plants, we encounter many more of these clever solutions.

We have only touched on the tiniest sampling of such solutions in the examples explored in this chapter. We've dipped a toe in an ocean of ingenuity, if you will—ingenuity that in our universal experience is wedded to a power unique to intelligent agents—foresight.

6. Birds: A Case Study in Foresight

The living world manifests numerous engineering solutions combined with ingenious chemistry far beyond the reach of unguided evolutionary mechanisms. A particularly striking example: birds. There are many aspects of bird biochemistry and architecture we could focus on suggestive of foresight, planning, and marvelous ingenuity. Here we will focus on just two aspects: bird navigation and bird reproduction.

Birds' GPS System

Migrating birds have out-of-this-world capabilities. Some birds, such as the common swift (*Apus apus*, Figure 6.1), have been reported to fly for ten months, during which they rarely and only briefly land while migrating from Europe to Africa and back again.[1] But perhaps even more impressive: They fly over long distances and diverse and changing landscapes without getting lost. It's as though they have a built-in GPS.

A human GPS (global positioning system) relies on the ingenuity of a mind and radio signals from artificial satellites orbiting the Earth. By integrating the signals from several satellites, a GPS can pinpoint its location on the Earth, sometimes within a few inches. Scientists have known for decades that birds have a GPS based on a more elegant principle: They sense the Earth's magnetic field.[2] The phenomenon is called magnetoreception.

Migratory birds navigate using this magnetic compass, but even non-migrating birds have this sense and navigate using their internal magnetic compass. It was once proposed that iron in birds' beaks pro-

Figure 6.1. The common swift (*Apus apus*) flies for months on its journey from Europe to Africa without getting lost. Part of its secret may be a cryptochrome molecule known as Cry4, so advanced it may harness quantum entanglement.

vided them with, in effect, a magnetic compass. It now appears that the sensor system is far more sophisticated: Special molecules in their eyes enable birds to *see* lines of the Earth's magnetic field (Figure 6.2) and use them as navigational guides.

The special molecules are highly sophisticated proteins called cryptochromes. Most cryptochromes are light-sensitive and are involved in the "circadian clock" that regulates the 24-hour metabolic and behavioral cycles in animals. But recent evidence suggests that one cryptochrome, designated Cry4, is involved in magnetoreception in birds.[3]

How might Cry4 detect magnetic field lines? When energized by light, Cry4 separates the electron from one of its electron pairs, forming what is called a "radical pair." (In vertebrates, cryptochromes are the only molecules that do this.) In an atom or molecule, an "orbital" is a specific quantum state that defines the energy, spin, and probable location of an electron relative to the nucleus. Normally, each orbital contains a pair of electrons with opposite spins and oppositely directed magnetic fields. A radical is formed when a chemical species bears one unpaired elec-

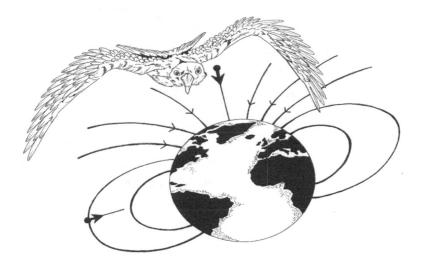

Figure 6.2. The common swift can in some cases fly for months at a time without landing, and navigates by seeing the lines of Earth's magnetic field, apparently by using the state-of-the-art Cry4 protein molecule in its eyes. Also impressive, it can fly and navigate while asleep.

tron, and a radical pair is formed when it has two unpaired electrons that are connected by what is known as quantum entanglement, one of the strangest phenomena discovered by modern physics.

As Dr. David Kaiser has elegantly described it, "Entanglement concerns the behavior of tiny particles, such as electrons, that have interacted in the past and then moved apart. Tickle one particle here, by measuring one of its properties—its position, momentum or 'spin'—and its partner should dance, instantaneously, no matter how far away the second particle has traveled."[4]

It sounds like science fiction, doesn't it? Albert Einstein, Boris Podolsky, and Nathan Rosen deduced this phenomenon from the theory of quantum mechanics, but they doubted it, concluding that the theory must therefore be incomplete.[5] But quantum entanglement was subsequently demonstrated experimentally. In 2013, a team of Chinese scientists showed that the communication between two entangled objects could not be less than 10,000 times the speed of light.[6]

It has been known for decades that radical pairs are affected by magnetic fields under laboratory conditions.[7] In 1996 chemists Brian Brocklehurst and Keith Alan McLauchlan suggested that the same phenomenon might occur in biological systems.[8] And in 2000 biophysicists Thorsten Ritz, Salih Adem, and Klaus Schulten proposed that the phenomenon might be the basis for magnetoreception in birds.[9]

When a radical pair forms in a light-activated Cry4 protein, the two members of the pair are only a few billionths of a meter away from each other. But even at this small molecular distance the two unpaired electrons could be affected differently by the Earth's magnetic field. Theoretically, many such entangled pairs could produce a picture in the bird's eye that enables it to navigate.

One problem for this proposal is that radical pairs connected by quantum entanglement are very short-lived. In a laboratory, the best molecule for maintaining quantum entanglement is a "Buckminsterfullerene," so named because it structurally resembles the geodesic domes designed by Buckminster Fuller in the 1940s. These beautiful carbon-based molecules are also called "buckyballs" or "fullerenes." Within a fullerene at room temperature, a radical pair in quantum entanglement can be maintained for about eighty microseconds.

In 2011, a team of physicists used "quantum information theory and the widely accepted 'radical pair' model to analyze recent experimental observations of the avian compass." The team concluded that quantum entanglement in the bird's eye lasts about one hundred microseconds, "exceeding the durations achieved in the best comparable man-made molecular systems."[10]

Physicist Simon Benjamin, a member of the team, put this in perspective by comparing the Cry4 protein to a fullerene. "How can a living system have evolved to protect a quantum state as well—no, better—than we can do in the lab with these exotic molecules?" he asked. "The bird, however it works, whatever it's got in there, it's somehow doing better than our specially designed, very beautiful molecule. That's just staggering."[11]

If a bird navigates through the Earth's magnetic field using radical pairs and quantum entanglement, it's implausible to suppose that such an amazing ability evolved one small, functional step at a time. The bird would have needed not only the ingenious magnetically sensitive molecules as sensors, but also the channels to transmit signals from the sensors to the right region of the brain. And the brain would have needed the apparatus to properly interpret and respond to that specific information. In order to provide a functional advantage, the entire "out of this world" system had to be implemented all at once. It seems therefore, as Fred Hoyle once concluded about our universe and life, that a "superintellect," capable of foresight, and of anticipating scientific discoveries, has "monkeyed" with quantum physics, along with chemistry and biology.[12]

Birds' Eggs

MOLECULAR OXYGEN (O_2) is necessary for life nearly from the moment of conception to convert nutrients into energy. No O_2, no life. A human baby needs O_2 even before the lungs start to work. As the fertilized human egg grows inside the mother's womb, the mother provides the baby with enough O_2 through the umbilical cord.

A bird embryo, in contrast, does not develop in its mother's womb. It is totally separated from its mother and isolated inside a capsule: the egg. From the outside, an egg looks more like a coffin than a cradle, enclosed by a hard, sealed, calcium carbonate ($CaCO_3$) shell. But an egg (Figure 6.3) is much more complex than it looks.[13]

But eggs, of course, are not coffins; they are self-contained cradles, full of weird and wonderful tricks to provide the chick with all it needs, from mechanical protection to a finely tuned package of food (the yolk and the egg white).

An egg is like a spaceship that contains all it needs, with one exception: O_2. At first glance, death by suffocation would seem to be inevita-

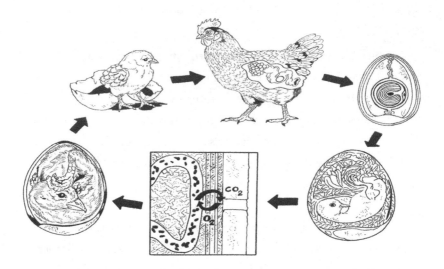

Figure 6.3. The biology of bird and reptile reproduction is unique, and scientists have long wondered how the highly sophisticated egg in the system originated.

ble. But the baby bird stays inside, maturing well, for weeks. How does it get oxygen? And how does it expel the carbon dioxide (CO_2) that results from converting nutrients into energy? If too much CO_2 were to accumulate inside, it would suffocate the baby animal. How does the chick selectively and efficiently get O_2 in and CO_2 out? NPR has a short online video on the subject that I highly recommend.[14] Here we will summarize much of what's described and depicted there.

Eggs have a hard yet water- and air-permeable shell, strong enough to bear the weight of an incubating mother. The shell contains thousands of tiny pores, each less than a thousandth of an inch across—too small to be seen with the naked eye. A chicken egg, for instance, has more than 7,000 tiny pores. These minuscule pores are perfectly calibrated to maintain the integrity of the whole structure. They deter invaders while allowing O_2 from fresh air to come in and waste CO_2 to get out. If the pores were either too big or too small, birds would have gone extinct.

But just having pores is not enough. Two remarkable selective membranes are located directly under the chicken egg's shell, which cooperate in a highly synchronized fashion. When the female sits on eggs to incubate her young, the eggs are usually warmer than the surrounding air. As an egg cools down, its contents shrink slightly, pulling the two inside membranes apart at the perfect moment. The shrinking sucks in air from the atmosphere, forming a small sac containing mostly nitrogen (N_2) but also sufficient O_2.

The baby bird then somehow "senses" that precious O_2 has entered the egg. To reach it, the chick develops a delicate network of capillaries in a precisely orchestrated genetic and metabolic process. These capillaries are perfectly engineered to move O_2 into and CO_2 out of the bird's blood. This network grows out of the chick's abdomen and presses up against the membranes, making close contact with them. The two membranes of the egg also allow selective permeation via proper exchange of O_2 and CO_2. It is a high-tech masterpiece of air treatment and control.

The egg pores are engineering masterpieces for another reason. They allow water molecules to move in and out of the shell. The water slowly evaporates, creating more empty space to fill with air. When the baby is ready to hatch, it punctures the inflated air sac to take his first breath while still inside the egg.

The egg tooth is yet another marvel of engineering. This tooth is a small horn-like projection that begins developing on the upper beak on the seventh day inside the egg. Hatching takes place twenty-one days after the egg is laid. As the time for hatching nears, it becomes hard and sharp so the chick can use it for breaking through the inner membrane to reach the air cell located in the egg's blunt end.[15] The air sac between the shell and inner membrane has just the right amount of oxygen to allow the chick to begin employing its respiratory system for up to three days before hatching. Using this air reservoir, the baby fills its lungs and gets strong enough to punch holes through the hard egg shell.

The chick's claws and beak aren't yet strong enough to break through the hard eggshell, so the egg tooth and the air sac are essential.[16] Without the egg tooth and the air sac, the chick would die inside the egg.

The baby bird also needs something else to make the first crack in the shell (called "pipping"). To break holes though the membranes and the hard shell, a pipping muscle swells on the backside of the bird's neck to press the beak against the shell. Punching an initial hole through the shell is so tiring that the chick rests for as much as eight hours afterward. Then, as Gail Damerow explains, the reinvigorated chick rotates itself counterclockwise, chipping the shell with its egg tooth "thousands of times, until it has broken the shell about three-quarters of the way around, creating a shell cap at the blunt end of the egg."[17]

This highly choreographed action of breaking an egg shell can take up to five hours. The chick knows when it is done and pushes against the shell cap with its head. After about forty minutes of labor, it finally breaks the shell cap loose. The newborn bird is exhausted again, and takes another rest. Finally, it gives one strong kick to escape the egg shell.[18]

The egg tooth is essential for the escape. But notice too that the chick's mother hasn't had the chance to teach the chick how to do any of this, and yet somehow it knows. (If it didn't, it would die.) This know-how also is part of what apparently must be foreseen and delivered in advance.

The chicks of some bird species, such as megapodes, don't have an egg tooth. Their egg shells are much softer, so they have no need to develop the nutrient-demanding tooth. They hatch feet-first to kick their way out, using sharp claws that have been ingeniously covered by jelly-like caps to avoid injuries. These jelly-like caps, like the egg tooth, fall off soon after the chick hatches.

There is an amazing synergy of action between the baby chick inside its egg and the mother outside. The mother hen "knows" she must incubate the egg for a few weeks, keeping it warm and turning it around several times a day. After about seventeen days of incubation beneath the mother hen, the chick starts to peep. Peeping signals the mother hen that the chick is almost ready to leave the egg.

As soon as she hears the message, the hen begins to peck holes in the rounded end of the shell. More air gets in, allowing the chick more oxygen and thus strength for hatching. From this point on, the chick will use its egg tooth to break the shell, ratcheting his body around in a very coordinated process until it can break free.

Though this is the commonest way for chicks to hatch, in a few species the chick splits the side of the egg and emerges through an untidy hole. The required amount of pecking varies, and appears pre-programmed to match the hardness of the egg and endurance of the chick.

Thomas Wentworth Higginson, a nineteenth-century author, abolitionist, and women's rights activist, once declared, "I think that, if required on pain of death to name instantly the most perfect thing in the universe, I should risk my fate on a bird's egg."[19] Multiple levels of foresight appear required to orchestrate such a perfect thing as an egg. As with other cases, the suggested evolutionary scenarios explain the benefit of having an egg and a chicken to provide it, but ignore the specifics of how this most exquisite system could have originated one small, blind step at a time over many generations.[20]

Which Came First?

THE AGE-OLD question is: Which came first, the chicken or the egg? It takes a chicken to make an egg, but it takes an egg to make a chicken. Without a chicken there would be no egg, but chickens that laid only partly evolved, not-fully-functional eggs would go extinct in a single generation—bye-bye, birdy.

A fully functional egg must be planned in advance, with correctly sized pores, inner membranes, and an expandable air sac. The chick must be programmed to connect itself via a network of blood vessels to the membranes, and to make its air sac slowly expand so the chick can exercise its new lungs before breaking the walls of its prison. The egg must also be loaded with just enough food for the chick to mature. The chick must have the strong and well-designed egg tooth and know how to chip out of its shell. The chick and the hen also must coordinate their behavior. If any of these intricate steps, behaviors, and structures were overlooked, birds would not survive long enough for natural selection to develop anything new. Birds and their eggs are, indeed, striking cases for foresight and planning in nature.

7. Foresight in the Human Form: Reproduction

O<small>UR OWN BODIES ARE SO FULL OF SOLUTIONS WHICH ANTICIPATE</small> complex problems that it would be remiss of me not to explore some of them in these pages. There are so many beautiful examples that I will cover just a small sampling of them.

Egg and Sperm

T<small>HE</small> <small>GREAT</small> miracle of conception begins with a mad dash. Between 100 million and 300 million sperm line up at the starting line (Figure 7.1). The finish line lies in the distance, and the prize is participating in the making of a new individual, a human baby. The winner is the first sperm able to penetrate the egg membrane. Such races can start several times a

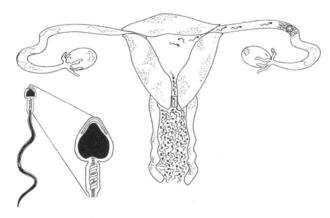

Figure 7.1. In the center is the human female reproductive system, with the vagina (lower part) filled with sperm. On the left is a sperm. Using their mitochondrial generators and their propellers, millions of sperm start the race, but only a single lucky one will find and penetrate the egg.

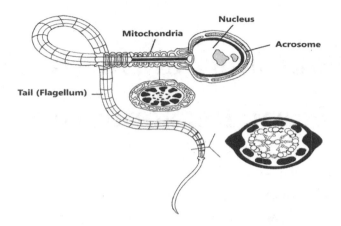

Figure 7.2. The most sophisticated race car on Earth: the sperm.

month, but many finish with no prize since an egg is waiting at the finish line only once a month.

The sperm is well equipped for the race with a long tail (called a flagellum, though it is very different from the bacterial flagellum) to propel it forward, several dozen mitochondrial power generators, billions of bytes of information to pass on, an "egg detector" to guide it, and a cocktail of enzymes to open its door to final victory.

Sperm constitute only a few percent of the volume of the seminal fluid, or semen, normally ejaculated by a human male. In their dash toward the egg, sperm need to be nourished, and semen nourishes them with the sugar fructose. Semen is also slightly alkaline, keeping the acid-sensitive sperm alive in the acidic conditions of the female reproductive tract.

The approximately 15-cm-long race track was also properly prepared. As the hormone estrogen is released, the physical barrier of the cervix opens, the cervical mucus grows more alkaline and watery, and uterine contractions are stimulated, helping the sperm to enter the reproductive system. To help the sperm reach the egg-bearing fallopian tube, uterine contractions come to the aid of the sperm's propulsion engine.

The sperm that make it to the cervical canal, escaping the attack of a defensive army of white blood cells, are rewarded by a sea of cervical mucus to transport them. This mucus is normally viscous, but exactly at the period of ovulation it becomes clear and thin so that the race track is properly paved with strings of molecules that sperm can ride to their final destination.

Once it's in the right place, how does the sperm find the egg? The sperm follows chemical attractants emitted by the egg,[1] using a chemical sensor that leads it toward the goal.

But the lucky sperm cannot win simply by being fastest. Some sperm will move too quickly and get there before the egg shows up. Others will be there too late. To make things even more difficult, there are two fallopian tubes, and usually there is an egg in only one of them.

All but a tiny fraction of the runners will fail to find the egg in the first place. Out of the millions of sperm at the starting line, only a few hundred will reach the egg. And reaching the egg isn't the end of the struggle. There is still the matter of penetrating the egg wall, the final challenge.

The egg is surrounded by a thick outer coating called the zona pellucida, which contains proteins decorated with branching carbohydrates. There are literally thousands of carbohydrate patterns the egg could have used to make these glycoproteins, as they are called, yet it makes only the kind the sperm recognizes. This perfect chemical match is necessary for success.

Necessary, but not sufficient. The sperm, having arrived, still has to make its way through the thicket.

Fortunately, the sperm is equipped with a mechanism to get past the zona pellucida. The head of the sperm is capped with a structure called the "acrosome." As soon as the acrosome contacts the zona pellucida, it

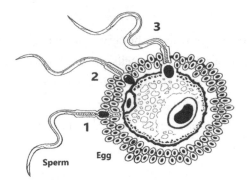

Figure 7.3. The most crucial moment comes when the winner finds the egg and breaks though its outer covering and membrane (steps 1 to 3) using an arsenal of ingenious enzymes. After that, the egg prevents all other sperm from entering.

releases just the right digestive enzymes to enable it to tunnel through the thick outer layer to reach the egg's membrane. (See Figure 7.3.) The membrane of the sperm then merges with the membrane of the egg.

And the egg doesn't stay still during the process. It moves toward the approaching sperm. The mucous membrane that lines the fallopian tube gives off secretions that help to transport both the egg and the sperm and keep them alive. Bicarbonates and lactic acid in these secretions are vital oxygen suppliers for the sperm and for developing the fertilized egg. Glucose is also present, providing a Red-Bull-like energy boost for both the egg and sperm. And a pool of properly designed chemicals provides an appropriate environment for fertilization.

The many aspects of this race for life are a marvel of orchestration. The chemistry and pH levels must be perfectly balanced. After the "first night," the uterus must be ready for the fertilized egg to implant. Implantation of the fertilized egg causes a programmed change in the hormones the woman's body produces—for example progesterone triggers development of the breasts. Then later, elevated estrogen levels in the blood prepare the breasts for lactation (along with other hormones such as luteinizing hormone).

But perhaps the most spectacular supporting cast members in the race of life are those in the mucous membrane. Propelled by nanomolecular engines, fine hair-like structures called cilia drag the egg through the fallopian tubes using highly synchronized movements like those of the arms and legs of a champion swimmer. This synchronized swimming motion, together with rhythmic muscular contractions of the wall of the fallopian tube, plus the flagellar propulsion of the sperm, moves sperm and egg toward each other.

The old saying, "Two's company; three's a crowd" is true here. The implantation should be a single egg with a single sperm, but scores of other sperm also make it to the egg and will try to crash the party. If two sperm penetrate the egg, the ensuing genetic chaos dooms the embryo.

To prevent this tragedy, a series of ingeniously orchestrated biochemical processes occur as soon as the sperm enters the first wall.[2] An army of soldier molecules quickly harden the outer egg wall as soon as the first sperm enters, preventing other sperm (not too many by now) from following. Penetration of a sperm and its fusion with the egg triggers the release of millions of calcium ions. These cause the cortical granules inside the egg and the plasma membrane to fuse. The cortical granules drop their payload outside the cell, enzymes that digest the zona pellucida, such that it can no longer bind sperm. Meanwhile, other molecules from the granules generate a new barrier layer around the fertilized egg. In this way, the deadly situation of a single egg being fertilized by multiple sperm is prevented.[3]

Recently, scientists solved a long-standing mystery in biology[4] when they discovered that a matching pair of specific proteins allows sperm to "dock" with an egg. The Juno protein, named for the Roman goddess of fertility, is situated on the surface of the egg and binds with a sperm-specific protein known as "Izumo," named for a Japanese shrine to marriage. How did they learn this amazing, coded trick?

This carefully coordinated process must occur perfectly for a human life to even *begin*. Everything must happen in order, nothing must go wrong, each piece must play its part, or there is no new human. If even one of the indispensable steps fails to work, no new life. It's all or nothing. Do you have any idea, or have you ever read a scientific paper, explaining in molecular terms—supported by data—how such a process could possibly come together one small, blind evolutionary step at a time? Don't feel bad. No one has. The reason for that, I would suggest, is that in reality it came together not through blind evolution but through foresight and careful preparation. That is the best explanation, given the growing wealth of evidence.

And the intricate necessities of a pre-born human do not end after implantation. Once this first, carefully coordinated stage is over, a nine-month-long journey begins—one that requires even more carefully synchronized parts and processes if a living, breathing infant is to be born.

The Chemical Arsenal of Pregnancy Hormones

As WE have briefly touched on above, pregnancy requires a concatenated series of chemical and morphological changes. These steps are triggered by a series of chemical messengers, a cocktail of fantastic biomolecules large and small, known together as hormones (Figure 7.4). They control and synchronize the production of an egg, its fertilization, the development of the embryo, and the child's final delivery from the mother's womb.[5]

Hormones are intriguing shapes from a chemical point of view. They are a special and structurally diverse set of chemical messengers that control most major body functions, from the basic processes that generate hunger to highly complex and sophisticated operations such as reproduction. Hormones even contribute to emotions and mood. One could write another entire book on the foresight manifested just in pregnancy hormones and other biomolecules that must have been present for the arrival of the first baby born on Earth. We'll look at just a small (if striking) set of examples here.

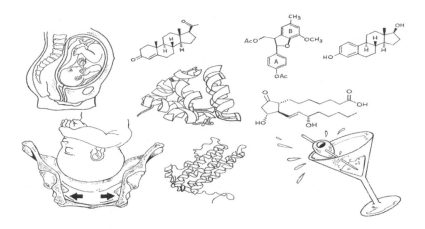

Figure 7.4. Just a sampling of the diverse cocktail of messenger biomolecules, or hormones, needed to orchestrate pregnancy and labor.

The various chemicals involved in pregnancy trigger specific pregnancy events, but also prevent problems that would otherwise kill the infant. Though some hormones play larger roles in pregnancy, all of them are necessary to produce a healthy baby. Here is a short list of hormones and a summary of their roles:

FSH: The follicle-stimulating hormone (FSH) is believed to be the first in the cascade of pregnancy hormones and is present in the mother's blood even before fertilization. FSH stimulates one of the egg-bearing follicles of the ovary, telling it to ripen and start making the hormone estrogen.

LH: The luteinizing hormone (LH), working in concert with FSH, orchestrates the menstrual cycle and becomes inactive during pregnancy. As FSH triggers production of estrogen, this messenger sets off an LH surge that commands the dominant follicle to release the egg from the ovary. The egg then migrates toward the fallopian tube, where it waits for the winning sperm to arrive. The splayed-apart follicle forms the corpus luteum, which disintegrates in about two weeks if an embryo fails to implant. If the egg is fertilized, the corpus luteum continues to grow, producing enough hormones to nourish and support the new life.

*h*CG: The human chorionic gonadotropin hormone (hCG) is the "just-for-pregnancy" messenger that triggers the production of estrogen and progesterone as soon as the egg is fertilized. Like LH, hCG is responsible for keeping the corpus luteum alive until the placenta takes over. Just as crucial, hCG suppresses that part of the mother's immune system that might mistake her baby as a foreign body and eliminate it. The newly developing placenta produces hCG just a few days after the fertilized egg implants to "fool" the mother's molecular army. The embryo checks in and stays for forty weeks, feeding off her nutrients. The amount of hCG is so high during pregnancy that it can be measured by home pregnancy tests. This hormone also stimulates the corpus luteum to produce more estrogen and progesterone. They rise and decline, but levels of hCG remains present throughout pregnancy, always on duty to protect the baby from rejection by the mother's immune system.

Estrogen: This hormone is there to do a lot of tasks, but mainly it helps the uterus grow, while regulating the production of other key hormones and triggering the development of the baby's organs.

Progesterone: This is a multi-function hormone that triggers the growth of breast tissue and, most importantly, helps soften ligaments and cartilage to prepare the mother's body for labor, so the baby can get out easier.

Relaxin: This is also a crucial hormone for pregnancy. Without relaxin, all the hard work would be in vain and the baby would be trapped inside the mother's womb. But this catastrophe was anticipated, and the proper solution provided: Relaxin sends a message to the mother's body to relax muscles, bones, ligaments, and joints to allow dilation of the cervix so the baby can be born.

*h*PL: Human placental lactogen (hPL) is the hormone responsible for sending messages to the mother's breast, making it ready for breastfeeding.

Oxytocin: This hormone triggers muscle contractions that coordinate labor for the baby's delivery. It also stimulates the nipples for breastfeeding and is known as the "love hormone," since it helps the mother bond with her new baby.

Prolactin: This is another amazing messenger for pregnancy. It triggers the increase in size of the mother's breast so it can produce sufficient milk for her newborn. (It's now well established, by the way, that mother's milk is better for babies than even the most advanced artificial baby formula.)

Without this fine-tuned cocktail of pregnancy hormones, there would be no newborns, because after implantation a baby would never reach the point of delivery.

Opening the Door: Cervical Dilation

THE CERVIX is the lower part of the uterus that opens into the vagina. As the baby develops in the uterus during pregnancy, the cervix serves two critical functions. First, it remains hard and unmoving during the forty weeks of pregnancy. The cervix serves to hold the developing fetus inside the uterus until the baby is mature enough for delivery. But precisely at the time for labor and delivery, a metabolic marvel occurs: The hypothalamus sends molecular messengers to the cervix to tell it the time has come for it to soften and become more elastic.

One might posit that cervix ripening was a selective advantage acquired over many generations of blind evolution, but notice the problem. If in the first-ever baby delivery, the cervix was not able to hold the baby in place and then open at exactly the right time, this poor pioneer infant would have been expelled too early or been trapped inside the mother's womb, leading to the death of both child and mother. No first baby, no chance for gradual evolution over many generations. Proper dilation at the right time of the cervix is a prerequisite for human reproduction.

During delivery, the cervix widens considerably from its normal diameter (which is 1–3 centimeters) to make room for the baby to come out. It is normally roughly cylindrical, long, and thick, but during delivery, the cervix shortens, thins, and pulls up into the lower part of the uterus, allowing it to open. This incredible widening, from 1–3 centimeters to up to ten centimeters, creates a passage for the baby's head and the rest of his body into the vaginal canal.

This dilation process can happen overnight, or gradually over a couple of days. Remember that the ripening of the cervix is stimulated by the hormone oxytocin, with the help of the high levels of estrogen. This stimulus in turn releases a group of additional hormones, known as prostaglandins (P2 and PGE2), which together play an indispensable role in dilation and labor.

Occasionally, inappropriate cervix dilation leads to complications in a baby's delivery.[6] Before modern medicine, these complications often led to the death of both mother and child. One might argue that this failure is evidence of the imperfect, trial-and-error process of blind evolution, rather than of foresight and planning by an all-wise designer. That's an objection with scientific, philosophical, and even theological dimensions. A whole book could be written on that, but here it suffices to note that it is a theological assumption that a good and wise designer would plan a world necessarily free of all pain, suffering, and death. Leading theological thinkers from various religious traditions have offered forceful arguments to the contrary.

But setting aside theological considerations, setting aside questions about the character of any would-be designer of nature, consider the following imaginative scenario. One day you discover a fleet of cars in a warehouse, all of them the same model. And this model is technologically far beyond anything humans have ever engineered. By comparison it makes a Formula 1 race car look like a horse wagon. Later you discover that some of these extraordinary vehicles have problems with clogged fuel lines. This failure would be interesting, and surely worthy of investigation, but hardly grounds for concluding that this amazing model of race car wasn't the work of foresight and planning.

Only if there were another, better explanation for the model's origin, one that accounted for all of the foresight and planning seemingly needed to build such a high-tech vehicle, *and* neatly accounted for the clogged fuel lines, would it be reasonable to even consider discarding the design explanation. And accounting for all the foresight and planning would require more than some vague stories starved of specifics.

For the extraordinarily sophisticated system that is human pregnancy and birth, the best no-design explanations—all modern variations on Darwin's theory of evolution—remain starved of specifics, leaning instead on all manner of hand-waving.

As for cervical dilation, it is a marvel that it works at all, works so often, and works so well. And once the baby is born, the cervix has one more trick, essential for the mother's health. As soon as the baby is out, the process automatically begins reversing itself, and the cervix soon regains its normal size and consistency, returning to its other function.

The need for both steps had to be anticipated. Foresee the need to ensure the developing baby stays inside the uterus, despite the mother's upright posture, then foresee the need for both cervical dilation and contraction at the right times, or no baby deliveries.

An Appendix: On the Appendix

BEFORE MOVING on to the next chapter, I would like to make a brief digression to look at an organ not involved in pregnancy, but no less a feat of anticipatory problem solving: the human appendix.

The digestive process is an essential part of human life. To provide us with needed nutrition, our digestive system and a wonderful pool of enzymes and nano-workers (intestinal bacteria) break large molecules from food into small molecules that our bodies can absorb and use for energy, growth, and cell repair. But sometimes there's a bug in the system—literally—and humans become ill and need to remove harmful substances from their digestive tract. This washing usually takes the form of diarrhea, which, while unpleasant, is necessary for our well-being.[7] When we get diarrhea, our body flushes out the bacteria that are making us sick. That is, cells in the wall of the intestine allow much more water than usual to enter it. By studying rats, scientists have discovered that this process is a masterpiece of chemical signaling, involving action triggered by a protein called interleukin-22 working with another protein, claudin-2.[8]

But as is often the case with even the most ingenious engineering solutions, the cure creates new problems. Diarrhea, while necessary, is not very selective. It eliminates the cause of sickness, but in the process, flushes out our good intestinal bacteria as well. These bacteria are essential for proper food digestion. So how does the body get around this dilemma? You may be surprised by the answer, because evolutionary theory has taught for years that the relevant organ was a useless leftover from evolution.

Our digestive system is made of an intricate array of interconnected organs: the gastrointestinal (GI) tract that extends from the mouth to the anus includes the liver, the pancreas, and the gall bladder, as well as the esophagus, stomach, small intestine, and large intestine. But tucked away in a corner off of our large intestine and isolated from the rest of the tract is a small, solitary, but rather important organ: the appendix, a finger-shaped sac attached to the cecum. (See Figure 7.5.)

Darwin and his followers assumed the appendix was a useless vestigial organ, left over from when we walked on four legs and ate a vegetarian diet. This evolutionary legend, based on lots of rhetoric and little evidence, has been around at least since Darwin argued for it in *The Descent of Man*.[9]

Although it sometimes annoys us, particularly in industrialized countries due to its modern susceptibility to inflammation,[10] we now know that the appendix performs at least two crucial functions (and hence is a valuable organ that you wouldn't want to lose unless it's absolutely necessary to remove it[11]). First, it is a source of antibody-producing blood cells and so a helpful part of our immune system.[12] Second, it acts as a safe house for good bacteria, repopulating the GI tract after diarrhea cleans it out.[13] Its location is perfect from a hydraulic engineering point of view: placed just below the normal one-way flow of food and germs in the large intestine, it occupies a *cul-de-sac* and is thus well protected from disruption due to diarrhea.

The appendix also appears to be useful during normal digestion, since, as highlighted in *Nature Reviews Microbiology*, it likely provides a "privileged anatomical" compartment for cultivating the good bacteria and protecting microbial inhabitants from competitors.[14]

So the Darwinian argument that the appendix is a vestigial organ that supports evolutionary theory is itself vestigial, a leftover of nineteenth-century Darwinian biology. We know better now.

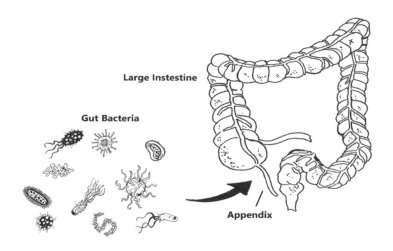

Figure 7.5. The human appendix, mistakenly regarded as a vestigial organ, has been discovered to work as a reservoir for essential bacteria.

8. Planning for the Senses

L ET'S LOOK NOW AT THE SENSES OF SIGHT, SMELL, AND TASTE, OUR capacity to feel pain, and an internal sensor crucial for breathing. Mostly we will focus on human senses, but just to keep ourselves humble, we will pause along the way to admire a champion sniffer from the order of insects, the humble moth.

Human Eyes

I'D BE remiss if I wrote a book about the evidence for foresight in biology and failed to explore one of the most compelling evidences of it—namely, sight.

Visible light is a collection of electromagnetic waves with wavelengths ranging from about 380 to 740 nanometers. (A nanometer is one billionth of a meter.) When visible light strikes an object, or passes through a gas, it is absorbed, reflected, refracted (bent), or scattered. When an object reflects all wavelengths equally, the human brain interprets the object as white. When the object absorbs them all equally, it appears black to us. When it absorbs some visible wavelengths and reflects others, we perceive it as some particular color, such as red, orange, yellow, green, blue, or violet. How we experience colors also has something to do with context. Everything from background colors to degree of familiarity plays a role.[1] There is an intimate relationship between colors and the brain's interpretation. Life very well might be viable in a shades-of-grey universe, but for some reason the universe is colorful and we are able to perceive a rainbow of colors.

The typical human retina (at the back of the eyeball) contains three types of cone cells—receptors that can distinguish three primary colors, plus millions of combinations. It also contains millions of receptor cells called rods that are more sensitive to light but can distinguish only black and white. As Jennifer Leong explains, in both cases, when light strikes a receptor, neural signals are created by chemical changes, and "these signals are then routed through neighboring bipolar and ganglion cells that form the optic nerve. This nerve then transmits information to the brain's visual cortex."[2] Eye sensitivity varies from person to person, but it has been estimated that humans with the best color vision can distinguish up to 10 million different colors.[3]

But just being able to perceive colors would be insufficient to aid survival. We also need a way to interpret what colors mean in everyday life.

The interpretation begins in nerve cells in the eye, but it is completed by the brain. Nerve signals from the eye are processed in the brain's visual cortex, which is so complex and integrated that it makes a modern computer look like an abacus. Developing this visual cortex required something utterly foreign to a random process: foresight. It took a *plan* to coordinate the integrated complexity that enables us to make sense out of what we see. The more you think about it, the more amazing it becomes.

Smell and Taste

IN MANY analytical laboratories worldwide, such as the mass spectrometry laboratories I oversee in Brazil, scientists have developed hundreds of different highly sensitive and selective instruments and methods to detect and identify chemicals. These methods help us understand the chemical composition of different types of aromas, drinks, and foods at as low as parts per trillion or less.

But long before the sensitive technology described above, people had to decide what to eat and not eat unguided by scientific knowledge. How did they make this essential decision? This ability to sort good food from bad food had to be there from the get-go. It's hard to imagine how this task could be acquired over a long time without life going extinct first. We have always needed to eat and drink, and we have always needed to know *what* to eat and drink. Imagine fishing in the morning and keeping the leftovers for dinner on a hot summer day without being able to recognize that the fish smells bad!

We have a clever solution to this problem. In addition to the analytical instrumentation in our eyes and visual cortex (far more sophisticated than artificial spectrophotometers for colors), we have analytical instrumentation in our noses, tongues, and brain that enables us to taste and smell with extreme sensitivity and accuracy—far beyond that of artificial mass spectrometers. And this biological instrumentation follows a general rule: Things that would make us sick or even kill us generally smell and/or taste bad. True, modern methods of food preparation have allowed us to refine, prepare, and eat way too much of some tasty foods that, eaten in moderation, would be fine for us but eaten to excess cause problems. And of course the system can be fooled, as evidenced by the existence of odorless and tasteless poisons. But the wonder is how well our senses of taste and smell generally steer us around deadly foods and toward foods that give us the healthy nutrients we need.

It has long been believed that human noses are somehow deficient. Aristotle wrote that "men have a poor sense of smell."[4] And Darwin erroneously concluded that a sense of smell was of "extremely slight service"[5] to the civilized human. These impressions, misguided by a false idea of how life works, reinforced nineteenth-century neuroanatomist Paul Broca's insistence that humans don't have a good sense of smell. It's true that dogs possess fifty times the olfactory receptors that humans have, meaning the strength of signal is probably stronger for dogs in many cases. Nevertheless, the healthy human nose possesses a sophisticated, built-in olfactory system[6] able to detect many thousands of scents and classify them as sweet, pungent, acrid, fragrant, warm, dry, or sour. Additionally, as John McGann notes, a recent study showed that "humans outperform laboratory rodents and dogs in detecting some odors while being less sensitive to other odors," and that "like other mammals, humans can distinguish among an incredible number of odors and can even follow outdoor scent trails."[7]

As McGann further explains, our olfactory bulb is large in absolute terms compared to mice and rats, and contains about as many neurons as the olfactory bulbs of other mammals. We therefore can "detect and differentiate an extraordinary range of odors," at least the ones that really matter to us.[8]

The connection between bad taste, bad smell, and bad food is so strong that we and most other animals (except scavenging birds, who have the digestive capacity to handle rotting carcasses) would starve to death rather than eat rotten meat. The rotten meat signal seems carefully planned, since it releases some of the most obnoxious and volatile molecules on Earth: two diamines that smell so strongly of death they were named cadaverine and putrescine.

The human tongue can detect five flavors: salty, sweet, bitter, sour, and umami—that is, savory. (According to recent research, humans might also be able to detect a sixth flavor: carbohydrates more complex than simple sugars.[9]) The nose and tongue team up with the brain to merge the taste and smell senses, and to detect the traces of scents and flavors too faint to be distinguished by themselves. We have much better taste and smell accuracy because our two human "mass spectrometers" work together in this way. As a paper in *Nature Neuroscience* explained, flavor perception is an integrative process activated "in two peripherally distinct neural systems, olfaction and gustation, which combine "to provide us with a unified oral sensation."[10]

Moths

ON THE scale of smell sensitivity, humans and dogs are impressive, but some of the best smellers are insects.[11] Among insects, male moths are "super-champions" that can smell highly specific sexual stimulants over long distances (Figure 8.1). Indeed, they can detect, amidst a myriad of other much more abundant molecules, a *single specific molecule* called a pheromone emitted miles away by a female moth.

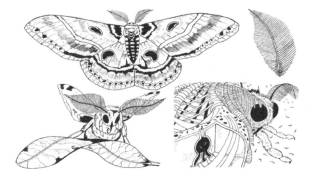

Figure 8.1. A chemical detector extraordinaire: the antenna of a male moth. Using a method of preconcentration sampling akin to solid phase micro-extraction (SPME), and employing what may be the most sensitive and selective detectors known to man, the male moth's antenna, scientists have shown, can detect a single molecule that has been emitted miles away by the female.

Male moths from several families accomplish this fully amazing task using an exquisitely designed sampling device: a highly sophisticated antenna with as many as 60,000 hair-like olfactory receptors. Its broad shape allows the antenna to come into contact with the largest possible volume of air for the greatest possible sensitivity in sampling.[12] The mechanisms that enable a male moth to detect incredibly low concentrations of pheromone molecules depend on a highly sophisticated set of proteins.

This highly sensitive and selective odor detection is, as Monika Stengl insists, "a prerequisite for survival and reproduction in many insects, especially in short-lived moths." The female moth releases a mix of pheromones to attract a mate. In a time-dependent synchrony with the female, the male moth hunts for the female's specific signaling molecules using a selective sampling and spectrometer-like device of "astounding sensitivity."[13] Both of these abilities had to be present for the potential mates to find each other and reproduce. One without the other is useless.

The male moth manages the job, Stengl writes, using specialized hair-like sensors on his antenna and can screen the air with molecule trackers pointing forward as it flies upwind. In doing so, it adsorbs around thirty percent of the lipophilic pheromone molecules in the surrounding air, thanks to the very selective waxy surfaces of its antenna. (This mimics how chemists sample trace substances using selective SPME fibers.) The male moth beats its wings at such a high frequency that the down strokes from its wings increase the airflow to improve SPME-like sample collection.[14]

Even if the female could produce the right blend of pheromones—a chemical miracle in itself—the pheromones would be useless if the male lacked the ability to detect them with extremely high sensitivity using the right sensors and SPME-like sampling. Building a system that allows male and female moths to find each other requires foresight at every step. Every strategy, the underlying biochemistry and biosensors, every bodily part involved, are a "primordial must" for the survival of the species. If any of these details were missing and, consequently, the male and female couldn't find each other, they would fail to reproduce and the species would soon become extinct.

Aggravating the problem, mature moths must reproduce during their very short lifetimes, so they must locate their partners very quickly. No time at all to wait for evolution over eons of time. Foresee and implement the right pheromones and the antennae at once, or goodbye moths.

Planning for Pain

OF COURSE, not all sensations are pleasant. Life is wonderful but quite often painful as well. Wouldn't a body that didn't experience pain be much better than the ones we have? Actually, pain is a feature of life extraordinarily valuable for survival. It protects us from noxious and dangerous stimuli, and losing the sensation of pain often results in injury and even death.

"No pain, no gain" is the rule at the gym. We could also say, no pain, no life.[15] The absence of pain would pose a fatal threat to life, because creatures would push themselves beyond the bounds of their strength without knowing any better, or ignore injuries until the injuries graduated from harmful to lethal.

Pain with properly tuned intensity is crucial to protect life.[16] For instance, when a boy steps on a nail, he feels intense pain through special pain-detecting nerve endings in his foot (nociceptors), which are perfectly located in skin and connective tissues. An electrical impulse is immediately transmitted to sensory neurons, and a nerve impulse is triggered and passed to the central nervous system through a relay neuron. Depending on the source of pain, this relay then directs the signal either to the brain or the spinal cord, and then back along the motor neuron to the muscles. The muscles quickly contract, limiting the injury and protecting the boy's foot, because he will immediately lift it when he feels the pain. If the boy grabs a hot pan, the muscles will recoil from the painful burning sensation in his hand. While the body is involved in many unconscious activities to minimize the threat, the conscious mind of the boy only feels pain and hopefully learns a lesson.

From the sting of a nail to the great agony of a shattered bone or burned skin, pain lets us know when we need to take action, tells us what part of our body needs attention, and motivates us to remedy it.

From experience we also learn that the intensity of the pain is calibrated to the level of injury, and that it only triggers a reflex stimulus when a damage threshold is reached. Imagine the agony if our pain sensors were not so well adjusted and we felt intense pain over trivial activities such as walking on gritty sand or receiving an overly enthusiastic hug.

Healthy people have no external organs that are immune to pain, and the most fragile organs are the ones that are most sensitive to it. Without pain, life would always be at risk. If the boy who stepped on the nail felt no pain, he would continue stepping further onto the nail, causing severe muscle and nerve damage, blood loss, and probably a serious infection. Pain informs him of the severity of the injury and stops him before he has time to consciously react. Without pain, we would put our lives and health at risk by engaging in dangerous activities without even realizing it.

To appreciate pain's purpose it helps to contrast it with congenital analgesia, a rare disorder that prevents individuals from feeling pain.[17] This potentially lethal pathology is caused by mutations[18] that damage several genes. As Mo Costandi reports, mutations in the *SCN9A* gene "produce a non-functional sodium channel, so that pain fibers can still detect painful stimuli but are unable to send the signals about them to the brain."[19]

This condition makes life a nightmare. People with congenital analgesia are vulnerable to serious cuts, fractures, and burns. It is so hazardous that those with the condition often die young because severe injuries or illnesses go unnoticed.[20]

The scientific literature reports several cases of children who were completely unable to sense physical pain of any sort from the day they were born.[21] Children suffering from this painless and horrible pathology begin chewing on their tongue while teething and also unconsciously mutilate their own fingers and lips. Their parents don't know to take them to the doctor when they contract appendicitis because the child never feels any abdominal pain, and so never complains. They burn themselves, or keep playing football on a broken ankle, or are bitten by ants or spiders without ever feeling a thing.

Evolutionists theorize that the sensation of pain was acquired slowly and by accident because it provided a survival advantage. And it is true that the history of life suggests a progression from less to more sensitive. For instance, cnidarians (such as jellyfish, sea anemones, and hydra) do have a very simple network of nerve cells that detect stimuli, most likely touch. Annelids have a somewhat more sensitive neural network that responds to touch, taste, and odor. Nociceptors are specialized neurons that some evolutionists would say are a short evolutionary distance from these other sensory neurons.

This is all worth noting, but the devil is in the details. What may seem a short distance from a distant vantage point may suddenly look very different when we draw closer and can discern the dauntingly sophisticated world of molecular biology, including its genetic and epigenetic information and information-processing systems. From this vantage point, suddenly the evolutionary pathway looks more like what Lewis and Clark must have witnessed after they reached the headwaters of the Missouri River and, rather than finding another river a hop, skip, and jump on the other side of the continental divide flowing west, they found mountain after mountain as far as the eye could see. Evolution's pathway is similarly much, much further away than initially assumed. And where the analogy breaks down is that evolution has no Lewis and Clark, or Sacajawea, for guides along the path—or for that matter, any goal. It is blind and purposeless.

Is the analogy otherwise a sound one? I predict that the more we learn about the molecular particulars of what differentiates our capacity for pain from that of more primitive life forms, the talk of an easy, breezy evolutionary walk from A to B to C to D will give way to an information-rich landscape of sophisticated and ingeniously orchestrated molecular machinery, with capacities that far exceed human-made machinery, ones with no plausible, detailed evolutionary pathway from primitive to sophisticated.

Breath or Death

WHEN WE think of senses we usually think of the big five—sight, hearing, touch, smell, and taste. But our body has many internal sensors that measure various factors key to our survival and send messages to our brain to keep them balanced. For example, our ability to breathe depends on a very sensitive detection system—a "sense" in one meaning of the word—that keeps track of oxygen (O_2) levels in our bodies. And that is just one enlightening example of a whole category of sensors and balancing mechanisms.

It's fortunate that O_2 is abundantly present in our atmosphere, for it is central to human life, and to practically all living things. But this doubly bonded diatomic molecule can, as noted earlier, also be harmful. O_2 is only beneficial to life forms that are prepared to use it in controlled ways, the specific means depending on the organism's level of sophistication and energy demands. Most life forms are armed with marvelous respiratory and blood-carrying systems that take O_2 from the air, carry it through blood vessels (using biomolecules such as hemoglobin) to where it is needed, and then bring the by-product back. We take in O_2 and eliminate its by-product, carbon dioxide (CO_2), by breathing constantly and at a well-controlled rate. It's a masterfully functioning, semi-automatic, silent, and smooth system, one that generally works so well we don't even think about it.

There, are of course, primitive outliers in this story. Cnidarians are in parts only two layers of cells thick, so every cell is exposed to the marine environment and obtains its own O_2. Earthworms simply absorb O_2 through their epidermis, which is why after a heavy rain they come to the surface, so they don't drown. There are, thus, multicellular animals that don't possess anything as intricate as what vertebrates have for processing O_2. Evolutionists would use these to tell a story connecting simple hydra up through the animal phyla and be quite sure of their evolutionary tale. But again, this would be another evolutionary "just-so" story, the two extremes connected by wishful thinking starved of molecular details—long on the *why* and short on the *how*.

We typically breathe between twelve and twenty times a minute, day in and day out, throughout our whole lives. Breathing consists of two phases—inhalation and exhalation. Our lungs continually expand and contract, supplying O_2 to our bodies and removing the waste CO_2. When you breathe in, your external intercostal muscles and diaphragm contract, pulling the diaphragm downward and moving the ribs up and out to expand the rib cage and our chest volume. The increase in chest volume lowers the air pressure inside the lungs compared to the outside air, drawing air in through our nostrils, mouth, larynx, and trachea. When we exhale, the external intercostal muscles and diaphragm relax, returning the thoracic cavity to its previous, smaller volume. This motion forces the air out of our lungs.[22]

The morphological design of our respiratory system includes bronchial tubes, which branch off from the trachea and then divide in the lungs into smaller air passages known as bronchioles. These end in over 300 million tiny balloon-like air sacs called alveoli, and surrounding each of these is a mesh of little blood vessels called capillaries. It is in these capillaries that the oxidizing O_2 passes through the alveoli walls and enters our blood. In the red blood cells the O_2 is loaded into a highly intricate molecule, hemoglobin. As the blood circulates throughout the body, hemoglobin releases O_2 to all the body's cells. The same hemoglobin then collects the waste CO_2 and returns it to the lungs, where it escapes into the alveoli and enters the air we exhale.[23]

All of these well-orchestrated processes usually happen automatically and unconsciously, controlled by our respiratory center in the brain stem, or medulla. Breathing continues even when we sleep, adjusted to the different O_2 requirements of resting. The medulla directs the spinal cord to maintain breathing while further smoothing of the respiration pattern is provided by the pons, located close to the medulla.[24]

The level of CO_2 in the arterial blood is used by the respiratory center to modulate breathing. CO_2 increases acidity, and if acidity increases, the chemoreceptors send a signal to the brain's respiratory center, which sends feedbacks to speed and deepen breathing. This process expels more CO_2 and brings in more O_2.[25]

If you are exposed to a suffocating atmosphere with too little O_2, such as the predominantly N_2 atmospheres inside a mass spectrometry laboratory, or at high altitudes while mountain climbing, or to an atmosphere with too much CO_2, such as the one in a corn silo, your metabolism will slow down to consume as little as O_2 as possible.

We can also observe our respiratory sensors in action in situations of reduced O_2 availability. When the O_2 concentration in our blood reduces, and CO_2 concentration increases accordingly, the normal flow of O_2 will be altered, and most of the blood flow from the limbs will be redirected to the two most critical organs: the brain and heart.

According to the findings of a study reported on in the journal *Cell*, the brain also appears to be equipped with a built-in chemometric sensor for atmospheric suffocation.[26] The amygdala—a vestigial (useless) organ according to misleading evolutionary predictions—is instead "part of the fear circuitry of the brain," John Wemmie of the University of Iowa explains, functioning as the suffocation sensor and stimulating the sympathetic nervous system.[27] Inhalation of CO_2 reduces brain pH, and the amygdala has an acid-sensing ion channel (known as ASIC1a)[28] activated by low pH levels. The findings demonstrate that the amygdala both senses the threat CO_2 poses, and triggers a response.[29]

Breathing is unusual among our bodily functions because it can continue on its own or be voluntarily regulated. Why should such a vital mechanism be susceptible to voluntary control? Conscious control of breathing rate and intensity allows humans to speak, sing, and play musical instruments such as the saxophone and trumpet. Breath control also allows us to swim.

But this ability to control our breathing comes with a price. If we didn't know when to stop holding our breath, we might easily damage brain and heart, and eventually organs would shut down and the brain die. So the brain's autonomous breathing control center quickly reasserts control and triggers the diaphragm into action. The urge to breathe triggered by our brain simply grows too strong, such that few can resist it while still conscious. And for the rare person who can, there remains a backstop: He faints, and then starts breathing again. The dictatorship of the brain in breathing saves us from auto-suffocation.

So next time you notice yourself breathing, pause and wonder at the marvelous design of our respiratory system. Without this delicate interplay of automatic, voluntary, and mandatory breathing via chemosensors and feedbacks in place, land-dwelling animals, including humans, would never have survived.

Conclusion

WITHOUT ALL of these delicate sense systems—and these really are just a few of the many possible examples—humans could never have existed. Also, these senses don't just allow us to survive. They allow us to experience and enjoy the world around us. These senses are absolutely crucial, and at the same time they are a gift that renders life both beautiful and compelling. This orchestration of senses looks for all the world like the result of careful planning, implemented before we ever knew we would need them or could understand their significance.

9. Foresight and the Future of Science

Time for a quick recap, and then let's step back and consider the implications of the evidence in these pages for the future of science.

The development of a chick embryo is a wonder to behold. (And you actually can behold it, because scientists have filmed the process.[1]) But no less a wonder than the developing embryo is the egg in which it develops. The egg yolk and egg white contain all the food the chick will need before it hatches. The eggshell also contains microscopic pores that let air in, so the chick can breathe. The developing bird then generates a network of capillaries to absorb oxygen from the air and release carbon dioxide. Just before hatching, special membranes in the egg trap enough air so the full-grown chick can take its first breath before it leaves the shell.

The eggshell is hard enough to protect the developing chick, yet fragile enough for the full-grown chick to peck its way out. Indeed, the egg's contents and shell are masterpieces of engineering that both nourish and protect the baby bird.

But there would be no egg without a chicken to produce it. Without an egg there can be no chicken, but without a chicken there can be no egg. It's the original *chicken-and-egg* problem, the archetypal example of a most curious causal circularity: To get A we need B, but to get B we first need A. We can't have one without the other. To get both together, we need foresight.

We find examples of this causal circularity—and thus the need for foresight—throughout living systems. As we have seen, living cells need membranes. No membranes, no life. And not just membranes, but membranes with a myriad of phospholipids and channels that enable a cell to control its internal environment. Those channels require complex and specialized proteins to function. Yet in the absence of a skilled biochemist, the necessary proteins are made only in cells—which existed long before there were biochemists. Without stable membranes loaded with protein-operated channels, there are no cells. But without cells there are no proteins to form membrane channels.

Or consider this: Inside a living cell we find DNA and RNA, both extremely well-suited for the jobs they perform—from the chemistry of their components to the chemistry of the complex molecules themselves. Without DNA and RNA, the cell could not synthesize the proteins it needs. Yet without a suite of complex proteins, the cell could not synthesize more DNA and thus could never divide. And without another suite of complex proteins, the cell would be unable to make RNA. No DNA and RNA, no proteins. No proteins, no DNA or RNA.

After proteins have been translated from RNA, chaperones help them to rapidly fold into the right three-dimensional shapes. Without the right shape, a protein cannot function properly. But chaperones are made of protein. Once again, we have causal circularity. No chaperones, no proteins. No proteins, no chaperones.

And it's not just causally circular systems that require foresight. The way bacteria cage and use poisonous hydrazine to convert nitrogenous waste and replenish atmospheric nitrogen; the way *Issus* insects use precisely meshed gears to jump; the way the mantis shrimp stores up elastic energy to power its remarkable strike while protecting its hands with gloves; the way birds use quantum entanglement to sense the Earth's magnetic field to navigate when they migrate; the coordination between sperm and egg in human reproduction; the way the appendix functions to replace beneficial bacteria in the digestive system after diarrhea; the integrated complexity involved in the senses of sight, smell, and pain: All of these point to the need for foresight.

Blind Man's Bluff

IN THE opening chapter I mentioned that evolutionists have made additions and other adjustments to Neo-Darwinism's central mechanism of random genetic mutations and natural selection. Some have gone so far down this path as to give up on the modern Neo-Darwinian synthesis even while clinging to the hope that some purely blind, materialistic version of evolution can be developed. The ongoing search for such an alternative to Neo-Darwinism was the subject of a 2016 meeting of the Royal Society of London, which included several distinguished evolutionists. The various proposals to salvage evolutionary theory—some more fashionable and some less—include punctuated equilibrium, neutral evolution (non-adaptive evolution), evolutionary developmental biology (evo-devo), self-organization, epigenetic inheritance, and natural genetic engineering. Big claims are made for each of these and other versions of blind evolution, but in the end those claims, while undoubtedly believed sincerely by their proponents, have little more substance than a bluff. Each has serious shortcomings as a substitute for foresight and planning.

Punctuated equilibrium, for example, attempts to explain why we see few transitional fossils in the fossil record from one animal form to a fundamentally different animal form, but it offers no credible mechanism for the geologically rapid evolution of new forms. Indeed, whatever challenges that traditional Neo-Darwinism faces in this regard, punctuated equilibrium faces them in intensified form, since it has less geological time to build new form.

Neutral evolution de-emphasizes the role of natural selection and focuses on mutations that, at least for a long time, would have been neutral or even deleterious in terms of fitness. The idea is that such mutations might predominate in small populations of, say, animals. The benefit of this approach is that evolutionists no longer have to envision a series of functionally advantageous steps from some starting point to the evolution of some new molecular machine, organ, or organism. But that benefit comes at an enormous cost, a cost its proponents tend to overlook.

Stephen Meyer, in discussing work on neutral evolution by Michael Lynch and Adam Abegg, explains with an illustration of a man dropped into a vast but happily predator-free body of water. (The lack of any predators in the analogy mirrors neutral evolution's de-emphasis on natural selection.) The man in the water just has to swim to a ladder somewhere in that vast body of water and climb out. The catch is that he's blindfolded and has no idea where the ladder is. Now, as Meyer points out, if you tried to estimate how long it would take him to reach the ladder by calculating a fairly direct line between man and ladder, you'd come up with "a fantastically optimistic estimate of the severity of the problem facing our unfortunate swimmer," because a straight line obscures the key problem the swimmer faces, namely that he has no clue where the ladder is, nor any way to gauge whether he's getting closer to or further from the ladder at any given moment. Meyer continues:

> Thus, any realistic estimate of how long it will actually take him to swim to the ladder—as opposed to an estimate of the theoretically fastest route possible—must take into account his probably aimless wandering, fits and starts, swimming in circles and drifting in various directions. Similarly Lynch and Abegg fail to reckon in their calculation on the random, undirected, and, literally, aimless nature of the mechanism that they propose. Instead, they mistakenly assume that neutral processes of evolution will make a beeline for some specific complex adaption. In fact, these processes will—in all probability—also wander aimlessly in a vast sequence space of neutral, functionless possibilities with nothing to direct them, or preserve them in any forward progress they happen to make, toward the rare and isolated islands of function represented by complex adaptations. For this reason, Lynch vastly underestimates the waiting times required to generate complex adaptations and, therefore, does not solve the problem of the origin of genes and proteins or any other complex adaptation.[2]

There is another problem. Not only is the neutral-evolution swimmer blindfolded, ignorant of where he needs to go, and without any desire to get there; there are other exits from this great body of water that lead to his destruction, or at least to a lost limb. That's because evolution does not go in one direction only. Mutations can break things much more easily than they can make them. Worse, this tendency for mutations to break will not politely sit on hold while neutral evolution casts about blindly for a mutation or series of mutations that build something new.

True, sometimes these devolutionary breaks lead to niche advantages, as Michael Behe discusses in his book *Darwin Devolves*. But as Behe also notes, no new molecular machinery has been built in such cases, and it's precisely the origin of new molecular machinery and information that any evolutionary account of the diversification of life needs to account for, neutral or otherwise.[3]

The other alternative evolutionary proposals face similarly devastating shortcomings.[4] What they all lack is the secret sauce in every great engineering success—foresight, ingenuity, and planning.

The Foresight-or-Death Principle

THE NEED to anticipate—to look into the future, predict potentially fatal problems with the plan, and solve them ahead of time—is observable all around us. It is clear from the many examples in this book that life is full of solutions whose need had to be predicted to avoid various dead-ends. Put another way, many biological functions and systems required planning to work. These features speak strongly against modern evolutionary theory in all its forms, which remains wedded to blind processes.

Also, as we saw in Chapter 2, the evidence of foresight in nature is not limited to examples from the life sciences. As we investigated Earth and the cosmos, we saw how it appears that an ingenious mind anticipated and steered around a host of potential dead-ends, in everything from physics and cosmology to chemistry and geology, situations that otherwise would have made life impossible.

No foresight, no life: In this book we have examined many instances that manifest this principle. And these barely scratch the surface. The many examples of solutions that anticipated problems before they arose, the ingenuity evident in those solutions, and the need for the orchestrated, simultaneous delivery of multiple, fully functioning components right from the beginning of a given system, pose a significant challenge to blind evolution. And not just blind evolution but the materialism that undergirds it, for foresight requires something more than matter in motion. Foresight is a hallmark of mind.

Foresight and Intelligence

WE HUMANS have thrived on Earth thanks to many of our unique abilities. We reason, possess the power of speech, craft sophisticated tools, grow crops, and breed livestock. We fly airplanes and spaceships and go deep into the oceans with submarines. We write software that commands mobile phones and robots. We synthesize polymers to make clothes, and drugs to cure us from pathologies. We sing, compose songs and plays, and much more.

What most sets us apart in the animal kingdom, then, is not something mechanical or material; rather, it is our minds. With our minds we can study the past, comprehend the present, and anticipate the future to a degree unparalleled in the animal kingdom. We, more than any other animal, foresee.

And yet, as we have witnessed throughout this book, acts of extraordinary foresight are evident throughout the natural world—in everything from cell membranes to the mechanisms of bird migration. And these examples far exceed in sophistication any examples of engineering foresight that we could point to in human culture.

Where does this evidence invite us? Let's take the case for foresight in nature in steps:

1.   We see many examples of apparent foresight in the natural world—of problems being anticipated before they arose, and

ingeniously solved with on-time delivery of multiple, essential, and well-orchestrated parts.

2. We know from our uniform experience that the ability to anticipate and solve such problems is a characteristic of intelligent minds.

3. There are no *demonstrated* examples of unguided, mindless processes anticipating and solving problems that require a sophisticated orchestration of fine-tuned parts, all brought together on the ground floor of an origin event. Hand-waving references to cases that are assumed rather than demonstrated do not count. Neither do arguments based on question-begging logic—e.g., "Common features must mean common descent" and "Common descent must mean blind evolution."

4. Therefore, our uniform experience provides us with only one type of cause with the *demonstrated* capacity to anticipate and solve such problems—intelligent design.

5. Intelligent design thus represents the best and, indeed, the only causally adequate explanation for the many examples of apparent foresight in the natural world, of situations where problems are ingeniously solved with on-time delivery of multiple, essential, and well-orchestrated parts. The foresight is not merely apparent, but real.

This isn't to say that there were no secondary causes in action, that nothing unfolded from law-like patterns and pre-existing conditions. Being open to the evidence of foresight leaves us open to consider both primary and secondary means. In each case under consideration we can simply follow the evidence rather than being constrained by a question-begging rule.

And whether the evidence points to primary causation, secondary causation, or a combination, it still follows that a mind was required to foresee the many potential dead-ends and escape them. Life and the universe are full of these clever escapes, ingenious solutions that speak strongly in favor of intelligent design.

Something More

I REMEMBER one dark night in a countryside fishing cottage in the city of Santa Fé do Sul, in Brazil. It was a clear night, and far enough from a large city that I saw, for the first time, the great spectacle that is the moonless night sky undimmed by urban light pollution—a vast multitude of sparkling stars.

I then asked myself, "Who made all of these uncountable stars and put them up there?" The impulse to attribute these wonders to someone is strong and nearly universal. But these days, that impulse is severely frowned upon.

But did the universe simply pop into existence out of nothing? No? Well, then, did a magical multiverse-generating machine pop out of nothing, itself fine-tuned to occasionally generate habitable universes? And whether we start with our universe or an imagined multiverse, did the fine-tuning of the laws and constants of nature just pop into existence?—lucky us! And from there did everything just blindly evolve right up to the first life on Earth—the first cell randomly bubbling up from some primordial soup? And from there the first multi-celled life, the first plants and animals, the first primates, the first human beings?

This is the atheist's creation story.

I must confess, as a chemist, I have too little faith to believe in such a religion.

We witness the beauty and intricacy of life on planet Earth, we behold the many amazing features that appear so carefully planned, and we are asked to believe that these wonders stumbled blindly out of the cold void, only to return to it one day. Is it true, as Carl Sagan intoned in priestly cadences at the beginning of his popular PBS series, "The Cosmos is all that is or was or ever will be"?[5]

Or is there something more?

Despite the wonders around us, for more than a century and a half many scientists have been convinced that the answers to such ultimate questions have been found, and that the marvels of the natural world are all due, as evolutionary biologist Francisco Ayala put it, to "chance and necessity jointly intricated in the stuff of life; randomness and determinism interlocked in a natural process that has spurted the most complex, diverse, and beautiful entities in the universe: the organisms that populate the earth, including humans who think and love."[6]

On this view, evolution provided design without a designer. We see evidence of purposive design in the universe and in us, but we are supposed to believe that this is just an illusion, and that, in reality, a process unguided by anything except the laws and constants of nature slowly formed all we know—the universe, the stars, the ocean, the sky and clouds, RNA and DNA, ribosomes, bacteria, fish, birds, chimpanzees, and us.

So we are told.

Sadly, this story has constrained science, narrowed our horizons, and deadened our wonder.

But happily, some fresh air has finally slipped onto the scene. The evidence of foresight and design in nature is growing progressively more apparent as we pursue scientific discovery. And unlike materialistic philosophy, an openness to the evidence for intelligent design broadens the horizons of science.

This book has described many clever mechanisms of life. But they are not merely clever. They are not just advantages that could have been acquired over eons of time through an evolutionary process; they are "primordial musts," features needed from the start for the organisms possessing them to survive and thrive. In each case, these solutions appear for all the world to have been planned in advance and present from the moment of take-off.

Modern evolutionary theory has little to offer in terms of explaining this *no foresight, no life* principle, since what is needed is anticipation and planning, and such activity is unique to minds.

After a long night of naturalism clamping down on scientific inquiry, the windows have been thrown open, questions new and old are being asked, and many of us find ourselves involved in a vigorous debate. Very good! Let the dogmas and suppression tactics retreat. We have two primary theories for our origins. Let the contenders stand up; let the evidence be presented; and let's deliberate and debate in a spirit of good will and fair play. May the theory that best explains the evidence win.

Such an open pursuit of the truth is, after all, a key element of what makes science exciting and fulfilling. I, for one, am glad to be living now, with new ideas, discoveries, and debates to enjoy.

What will be the outcome? I cannot say how quickly other scientists will be willing to follow the evidence where it leads, but I do know that those of us willing to heed the evidence of foresight in nature are participating in an intellectually fascinating and exciting scientific revolution. Powered by new tools of investigation and fresh discoveries about the world, this revolution is enriched by the revival of an idea with a royal pedigree: design. The fathers of modern science—Copernicus, Galileo, Kepler, Newton, Boyle, and many others—saw design in the universe and, indeed, were inspired to discover the laws of nature because of their belief in a transcendent law-giver.

As for that wondrous journey of discovery that they launched, there seems to be no end in sight. Nobel laureate J. J. Thomson—one of the giants of early modern physics, the discoverer of the electron, and the father of mass spectrometry, my field of expertise—beautifully conveyed this optimistic, open-ended view of science. I can think of no better words for concluding a book about a world filled with evidence of foresight, words as true today as when Thomson penned them in the early twentieth century:

> The sum of knowledge is at present, at any rate, a diverging, not a converging, series. As we conquer peak after peak we see in front of us regions full of interest and beauty, but we do not see our goal, we do not see the horizon; in the distance tower still higher peaks, which will yield to those who ascend them still wider prospects, and deepen the feeling, the truth of which is emphasized by every advance in science, that "Great are the Works of the Lord."[7]

ENDNOTES

1. FORESIGHT IN LIFE

1. Sheref S. Mansy et al., "Template-Directed Synthesis of a Genetic Polymer in a Model Protocell," *Nature* 454 (2008): 122.

2. Here I recall the intricacy of electronic temperature meters and pH meters used in my work as a chemist.

3. Diego de Mendoza, "Temperature Sensing Membranes," *Annual Review of Microbiology* 68, no. 1 (September 2014): 101–16, https://doi.org/10.1146/annurev-micro-091313-103612.

4. Jack W. Szostak, David P. Bartel, and P. Luigi Luisi, "Synthesizing Life," *Nature* 409, no. 6818 (2001): 387–90.

5. David J. Siminovitch, P. T. T. Wong, and Henry H. Mantsch, "Effects of Cis and Trans Unsaturation on the Structure of Phospholipid Bilayers: A High-Pressure Infrared Spectroscopic Study," *Biochemistry* 26, no. 12 (1987): 3277–87.

6. Sheref S. Mansy et al., "Template-Directed Synthesis," 122–5. See also Charles L. Apel, David W. Deamer, and Michael N. Mautner, "Self-Assembled Vesicles of Monocarboxylic Acids and Alcohols: Conditions for Stability and for the Encapsulation of Biopolymers," *Biochimica et Biophysica Acta (BBA) – Biomembranes* 1559, no. 1 (2002): 1–9.

7. Armen Y. Mulkidjanian, Michael Y. Galperin, and Eugene V. Koonin, "Co-evolution of Primordial Membranes and Membrane Proteins," *Trends in Biochemical Sciences* 34, no. 4 (2009): 206–15.

8. Mulkidjanian, Galperin, and Koonin, "Co-evolution of Primordial Membranes," 206.

9. Mario Borgnia et al., "Cellular and Molecular Biology of the Aquaporin Water Channels," *Annual Review of Biochemistry* 68 (1999): 425–58.

10. Kazuyoshi Murata et al., "Structural Determinants of Water Permeation through Aquaporin-1," *Nature* 407 (2000): 599–605.

11. Urszula Kosinska Eriksson et al., "Subangstrom Resolution X-Ray Structure Details Aquaporin-Water Interactions," *Science* 340, no. 6138 (2013): 1346–1349.

12. "Nobel Prize in Chemistry 2003," *The Nobel Prize*, Nobel Media AB, https://www.nobelprize.org/nobel_prizes/chemistry/laureates/2003/.

13. This phrase is from Richard Dawkins, *Climbing Mount Improbable* (New York: W. W. Norton & Company, 1996).

2. A WORLD FORESEEN FOR BIOCHEMISTRY

1. For more on the universal constants and the fine-tuned intricate universe they reveal, see: Ethan Siegel, "It Takes 26 Fundamental Constants to Give Us Our Universe, But They Still Don't Give Everything," *Forbes*, August 22, 2015, https://www.forbes.com/sites/ethansiegel/2015/08/22/it-takes-26-fundamental-constants-to-give-us-our-universe-but-they-still-dont-give-everything/#2209877a4b86.

2. See Geraint F. Lewis and Luke A. Barnes, *A Fortunate Universe: Life in a Finely Tuned Cosmos* (Cambridge, England: Cambridge University Press, 2016). For an older online summary, see Jay W. Richards, "List of Fine-Tuning Parameters," Discovery Institute's Center for Science and Culture, https://www.discovery.org/f/11011.

3. Fred Hoyle, "The Universe: Past and Present Reflections," *Engineering and Science* 45, no. 2 (1981): 8.

4. "The Peculiar Properties of Ice," *Evolution News & Science Today*, August 7, 2012, https://evolutionnews.org/2012/08/the_peculiar_pr_1/.

5. Preston Dyches and Felicia Chou, "The Solar System and Beyond Is Awash in Water," *NASA*, April 7, 2015, https://www.nasa.gov/jpl/the-solar-system-and-beyond-is-awash-in-water.

6. For a fuller exploration of water's near-miraculous properties, see Michael Denton, *The Wonder of Water: Water's Profound Fitness for Life on Earth and Mankind* (Seattle, WA: Discovery Institute Press, 2017).

7. A famous and controversial "memory of water" paper was once published in *Nature* and exemplifies how an appealing theory can be proposed and published in prestigious journals without much—if any—solid evidence. The paper reported the why and when but neglected to address the critical question of how. The paper: E. Davenas et al., "Human Basophil Degranulation Triggered by Very Dilute Antiserum against IgE," *Nature* 333, no. 6176 (1988): 816–8.

8. For a detailed online discussion of water's many life-friendly anomalous properties, see Martin Chaplin, "Anomalous Properties of Water," Water Structure and Science, http://www1.lsbu.ac.uk/water/water_anomalies.html. For a brief online discussion, see Steven Dutch, "Ice Floats," Intelligent Design. Intelligently, http://www.stevedutch.net/Pseudosc/IntelIntel.htm. Dutch makes several good points, though he mischaracterizes design theory near the end of the section. He writes: "So why don't Intelligent Designers say much about the remarkable properties of water? Well, the fact that water not only organizes into a structure when it freezes, but actually does so strongly enough to force things to give it room, sort of blows a large hole in their claim that order can't arise from natural processes." But "Intelligent Designers" actually *have* made a big deal about the remarkable properties of water. Guillermo Gonzalez and Jay Richards, both ID proponents, did so in their book *The Privileged Planet*, published three years before Dutch created the page. More recently, Discovery Institute, an institutional hub for scientists and scholars exploring and advocating the theory of intelligent design, published a book on the subject, *The Wonder of Water* by Michael Denton. Further, the theory of intelligent *doesn't* posit that order can't arise from natural processes. William Dembski, for instance, in his 1998 Cambridge University Press book *The Design Inference*, and in many subsequent intelligent design works, draws a distinction between the periodic order of such things as crystals and whirlpools, on the one hand, and on the other hand, what he terms *complex specified information* (CSI)—which is non-random but also aperiodic—such as we find in human language, computer software, and DNA. Generating significant amounts of novel CSI through blind natural forces—that's what design theorists argue doesn't happen. More on the wonders of DNA in a later chapter.

9. Dutch, "Ice Floats."

10. Sand to M. Charles Poncy, September 12, 1844, in *Letters of George Sand: Vol. 1*, trans. Raphaël Ledo de Beaufort (London: Ward and Downey, 1886), 355.

11. For a discussion of some of these factors, see Bess B. Ward and Marlene M. Jensen, "The Microbial Nitrogen Cycle," *Frontiers in Microbiology* 5 (2014): 553.

12. Asta Juzeniene and Johan Moan, "Beneficial Effects of UV Radiation Other Than via Vitamin D Production," *Dermato-Endocrinology* 4, no. 2 (2014): 109–117.

13. "Ozone: Good Up High, Bad Nearby," Office of Air and Radiation, U.S. Environmental Protection Agency, June 2003, https://www3.epa.gov/airnow/gooduphigh/ozone.pdf.

14. Fakhra Anwar et al., "Causes of Ozone Layer Depletion and Its Effects on Human [Health]: Review," *Atmospheric and Climate Sciences* 6 (2016): 129–134.

15. David L. Drapcho, Douglas Sisterson, and Romesh Kumar, "Nitrogen Fixation by Lightning Activity in a Thunderstorm," *Atmospheric Environment* 17, no. 4 (1983): 729–734.

16. Martin A. Uman, "Natural Lightning," *IEEE Transactions on Industry Applications* 30, no. 3 (1994): 785e90.

17. V. A. Rakov, "The Physics of Lightning," *Surv Geophys* 34 (2013): 701–729.

18. Donald E. Canfield, Alexander Glazer, and Paul G. Falkowski, "The Evolution and Future of Earth's Nitrogen Cycle," *Science* 330, no. 6001 (2010): 193.

19. E. E. Ferguson and W. F. Libby, "Mechanism for the Fixation of Nitrogen by Lightning," *Nature* 229 (1971): 37.

20. David Fowler et al., "The Global Nitrogen Cycle in the Twenty-First Century," *Philosophical Transactions of the Royal Society B: Biological Sciences* 368, no. 1621 (2013): 1.

21. Fowler, "The Global Nitrogen Cycle," 1–2. As they further note, NO_x molecules also play key roles "in the photochemical production of ozone and other key oxidants and radical species." See also J. N. Galloway et al., "Nitrogen Cycles: Past, Present, and Future," *Biogeochemistry* 70, no. 2 (2007): 153–226; Richard P. Wayne, *Chemistry of Atmospheres* (Oxford: Clarendon Press, 1991); I. S. A. Isaksen, et al., "Atmospheric Composition Change: Climate–Chemistry Interactions," *Atmosphere Environment* 43, no. 33 (2009): 5138–5192.

22. Fowler, "The Global Nitrogen Cycle," 2.

23. Andrei Linde, "Multiverse: A Brief History of the Multiverse," *Reports on Progress in Physics* 80, no. 2 (2015).

24. For an in-depth exploration of fine tuning and the case for and against the multiverse solution to the fine-tuning problem, see Lewis and Barnes, *A Fortunate Universe*.

25. For an extended case that planetary and cosmological fine tuning is best explained by reference to an intelligent cause, see Guillermo Gonzalez and Jay W. Richards, *The Privileged Planet: How Our Place in the Cosmos is Designed for Discovery* (Washington, DC: Regnery, 2004).

26. Nancy R. Pearcey and Charles B. Thaxton, *The Soul of Science: Christian Faith and Natural Philosophy* (Wheaton, IL: Crossway Books, 1994).

27. Kansas State Department of Education, Standards Development Committee, *Kansas Science Education Standards*, February 2007, xii, http://www.rv337.com/pages/uploaded_files/sci_standards_Aug07b.pdf.

28. Gary J. Nabel, "The Coordinates of Truth," *Science* 326, no. 5949 (2009): 53–54.

3. THE CODE OF LIFE

1. Manfred Eigen et al., "How Old is the Genetic Code? Statistical Geometry of tRNA Provides an Answer," *Science* 244, no. 4905 (1989): 673–79.

2. Feng Yue et al., "A Comparative Encyclopedia of DNA Elements in the Mouse Genome," *Nature* 515 (2014): 355–364. By some estimates, genomes differ only between 3% and 8% from one mammal species to another. This may be true for mammals, but not for other species. A detailed examination of fruit flies, for instance, revealed "that only 77% of the approximately 13,700 protein-coding genes in *D. melanogaster* are shared with all of the other eleven species." Quoted from "Scientists Compare Twelve Fruit Fly Genomes," National Institutes of Health, November 7, 2007, https://www.nih.gov/news-events/news-releases/scientists-compare-twelve-fruit-fly-genomes.

3. There are widely varying estimates for the percentage of genetic information shared in common between humans and bananas. For the 60% figure, see Lydia Ramsey and Samantha Lee, "Our DNA is 99.9% the Same as the Person Next to Us—and We're Surprisingly Similar to a Lot of Other Living Things," *Business Insider*, April 3, 2018, http://www.businessinsider.com/comparing-genetic-similarity-between-humans-and-other-things-2016-5.

4. F. H. Westheimer, "Why Nature Chose Phosphates," *Science* 235, no. 4793 (1987): 1173–1178.

5. Ryszard Kierzek, Liyan He, and Douglas H. Turner, "Association of 2'-5' Oligoribonucleotides," *Nucleic Acids Research* 20, no. 7 (1992): 1685–1690.

6. Shina C. Kamerlin et al., "Why Nature Really Chose Phosphate," *Quarterly Reviews of Biophysics* 46, no. 1 (2013): 1–132, https://www.ncbi.nlm.nih.gov/pubmed/23318152.

7. Gaspar Banfalvi, "Why Ribose Was Selected as the Sugar Component of Nucleic Acids," *DNA Cell Biology* 25, no. 3 (2006): 189–96.

8. James Tour, "Animadversions of a Synthetic Chemist," *Inference: International Review of Science*, 2.2 (May 2016), https://inference-review.com/article/animadversions-of-a-synthetic-chemist.

9. Stephen J. Freeland and Laurence D. Hurst, "The Genetic Code is One in a Million," *Journal of Molecular Evolution* 47 (1998): 238–248. Note that for the DNA with its deoxyribose sugar, the 2'-OH group was removed, so DNA hydrolysis is no longer assisted by a favored intramolecular TS, and the attack of a base must therefore come from "outside." DNA is well-protected from hydrolysis since it is fully surrounded by an electrical shield provided by the phosphate anion wire discussed earlier.

10. Gerald F. Joyce, "The Antiquity of RNA-Based Evolution," *Nature* 418 (2002): 214–221. How does the apparently "silent" 2'-OH group help RNA undergo hydrolysis about one hundred times faster than DNA? It's a marvel of engineering. Via a cyclic intermediate, with intramolecular assistance from the OH group at the 2' position of the ribose cycle (nanometrically calibrated to be there), a six-membered transition state is formed when a base, in an alkaline medium, attacks it, removing its acidic proton. This forms an alkoxy anion intermediate, which then intramolecularly attacks the phosphate wire in a well-coordinated SN2 mechanism, breaking the wire and therefore "digesting" RNA.

11. Philip Ball, "DNA: Celebrate the Unknowns," *Nature* 496 (2013): 419–420.

12. "Why Did Mother Nature Use Uracil to Replace Thymine in mRNA (Messenger Ribonucleic Acid)? What Is the Advantage of Using U Instead of T in the RNA?" *NSTA Web-*

News Digest, National Science Teachers Association, September 16, 2006, http://www. nsta.org/publications/news/story.aspx?id=52606.

13. A. M. Lesk, "Why Does DNA Contain Thymine and RNA Uracil?" *Journal of Theoretical Biology* 22, no. 3 (1969): 537–40; Greg A. Freyer and Michael Sturr, "Why Did Mother Nature Use Uracil to Replace Thymine." (Note that the citation of this article in the previous endnote (sans Freyer and Sturr) is to a statement from the digest editors further setting up the question that Freyer and Sturr answer in their responses.)

14. Michael Onken, "Why Does Uracil Replace Thymine in RNA?" MadSci Network, November 11, 1997, http://www.madsci.org/posts/archives/dec97/879354206.Bc.r.html.

15. Jörgen Jonsson, Maria Sandberg, and Svante Wold, "The Evolutionary Transition from Uracil to Thymine Balances the Genetic Code," *Journal of Chemometrics* 10, no. 2 (1996): 163.

16. Beáta G. Vértessy and Judit Tóth, "Keeping Uracil Out of DNA: Physiological Role, Structure and Catalytic Mechanism of dUTPases," *Accounts on Chemical Research* 42, no. 1 (2009) 97–106.

17. Freyer, answer to "Why Did Mother Nature Use Uracil?" (cited above).

18. Walter Gilbert, "Origin of Life: The RNA World," *Nature* 319 (1986): 618.

19. David J. D'Onofrio and David L. Abel, "Redundancy of the Genetic Code Enables Translational Pausing," *Frontiers in Genetics* 5 (2014): 1.

20. Christina E. Brule and Elizabeth J. Grayhack, "Synonymous Codons: Choose Wisely for Expression," *Trends Genet.* 33:4 (2017): 283–97.

21. Thomas Charles Butler et al., "Extreme Genetic Code Optimality from a Molecular Dynamics Calculation of Amino Acid Polar Requirement," *Physical Review E* 79, no. 6 part 1 (2009): 060901.

22. "The Nobel Prize in Chemistry 2015," *The Nobel Prize*, Nobel Media AB, https://www. nobelprize.org/nobel_prizes/chemistry/laureates/2015/.

23. "The Nobel Prize in Chemistry 2016," *The Nobel Prize*, Nobel Media AB, https://www. nobelprize.org/nobel_prizes/chemistry/laureates/2016/.

24. Kelson M. T. Oliveira and Elaine Harada, "Synthetic Routes of the Fundamental Building Blocks of Life: Computational Study of the Reaction Free Energy," *Revista Processos Químicos* 18 (2015): 139–143, http://bkp.sbqt-2015.net.br/arquivos/Anais/RPQ_sbqt_2015_especial_12NovV2.pdf.

25. Gary Habermas, "My Pilgrimage from Atheism to Theism: A Discussion between Antony Flew and Gary Habermas," *Faculty Publications and Presentations*, Liberty University, 2004, 201, https://digitalcommons.liberty.edu/cgi/viewcontent. cgi?article=1336&context=lts_fac_pubs.

26. Francis H. Crick, "The Origin of the Genetic Code," *Journal of Molecular Biology* 38, no. 3 (1968): 367–79.

4. Life's Helpers

1. Sylvia S. Mader, *Biology: 10th Edition* (New York: McGraw Hill, 2009), 236.

2. A. Ralston, "Operons and Prokaryotic Gene Regulation," *Nature Education* 1, no. 1 (2008): 216.

3. James Shapiro, "A 21st Century View of Evolution: Genome System Architecture, Repetitive DNA, and Natural Genetic Engineering," *Gene*, 345, no. 1, (2005), 92–93.

4. Carl Zimmer, "Scientists are Designing Artisanal Proteins for Your Body," *The New York Times*, December 26, 2017, https://www.nytimes.com/2017/12/26/science/protein-design-david-baker.html.

5. Lars Giger et al., "Evolution of a Designed Retro-Aldolase Leads to Complete Active Site Remodeling," *Nature Chemical Biology* 9 (2013): 494–498.

6. F. Ulrich Hartl, Andreas Bracher, and Manajit Hayer-Hartl, "Molecular Chaperones in Protein Folding and Proteostasis," *Nature* 475 (2011): 324.

7. R. A. Quinlan and R. J. Ellis, "Chaperones: Needed for Both the Good Times and the Bad Times," *Philosophical Transactions of the Royal Society B* 368, no. 1617 (2013): 20130091.

8. Laurence A. Moran, "Protein Folding, Chaperones, and IDiots," *Sandwalk*, August 20, 2011, http://sandwalk.blogspot.com.br/2011/08/protein-folding-chaperones-and-idiots.html.

9. Susmita Kaushik and Ana Maria Cuervo, "Proteostasis and Aging," *Nature Medicine* 21, no. 12 (2015): 1406.

10. M. Beissinger and J. Buchner, "How Chaperones Fold Proteins," *Journal of Biological Chemistry* 379, no. 3 (1988): 245.

11. Antony Latham, "New Research on Protein Folding Demonstrates Intelligent Design," Centre for Intelligent Design, July 2011, https://www.c4id.org.uk.

12. Moran, "Protein Folding."

13. N. M. Lissin, S. Yu. Venyaminov, and A. S. Girshovich, "(Mg–ATP)-Dependent Self-Assembly of Molecular Chaperone GroEL," *Nature* 348 (1990): 339–342.

14. Satish Babu Moparthi et al., "Transient Conformational Remodeling of Folding Proteins by GroES—Individually and in Concert with GroEL," *Journal of Chemical Biology* 7, no. 1 (2014): 11.

15. Bruce Alberts et al., *Molecular Biology of the Cell: Sixth Edition* (New York: Garland Science, 2017), 355.

16. F. Ulrich Hartl et al., "Protein Folding," 326.

17. F. Ulrich Hartl et al., "Protein Folding," 325.

18. Moran, "Protein Folding."

19. Quinlan and Ellis, "Chaperones."

20. Quinlan and Ellis, "Chaperones."

21. Clyde A. Hutchison III et al., "Design and Synthesis of a Minimal Bacterial Genome," *Science* 351, no. 6280 (2016): 1414.

22. Koji Yonekura, Saori Maki-Yonekura, and Keiichi Namba, "Building the Atomic Model for the Bacterial Flagellar Filament by Electron Cryomicroscopy and Image Analysis," *Structure* 13, no. 3 (2005): 407–12. For more information on the exquisite structure of the flagellar filament, see also Saori Maki-Yonekura, Koji Yonekura, and Keiichi Namba, "Domain Movements of HAP2 in the Cap–Filament Complex Formation and Growth Process of the Bacterial Flagellum," *Proceedings of the National Academy of Science* 100, no. 26 (2003): 15528–33.

23. For more on the flagellar cap and how it suggests intelligent design, including an animated video, see Jonathan M., "The Flagellar Filament Cap: One of the Most Dynamic Movements in Protein Structures," *Evolution News & Science Today*, August 3, 2013, https://evolutionnews.org/2013/08/the_flagellar_f/.

24. Jonathan M., "The Flagellar Filament Cap."

25. D. F. Blair and K. T. Hughes, "Irreducible Complexity? Not!" in *Microbes and Evolution: The World That Darwin Never Saw*, eds. R. Kolter and S. Maloy (Washington, DC: ASM Press, 2012), 275–80; W. Ford Doolittle and Olga Zhaxybayeva, "Evolution: Reducible Complexity—The Case for Bacterial Flagella," *Current Biology* 17, no. 13 (2007): R510–2.

26. Jonathan M., "The Flagellar Filament Cap."

27. Kenneth R. Miller, "The Flaw in the Mousetrap: Intelligent Design Fails the Biochemistry Test," *Natural History* 75 (2002).

28. Shin-Ichi Aizawa, "What is Essential for Flagellar Assembly," *Pili and Flagella: Current Research and Future Trends* (Norfolk, UK: Caister Academic Press, 2009), 91.

5. BACTERIA, BUGS, AND CARNIVOROUS PLANTS

1. For more on the synergy of microbes and life, see: "How Microbes Make Earth Habitable," *Evolution News & Science Today*, February 10, 2016, https://evolutionnews.org/2016/02/how_microbes_ma/; "More on How Microbes Make Earth Habitable," *Evolution News & Science Today*, February 14, 2016, https://evolutionnews.org/2016/02/more_on_how_mic/.

2. J. Gijs Kuenen, "Anammox Bacteria: From Discovery to Application," *Nature Reviews Microbiology* 6, no. 4 (2008): 320–6. See also Andreas Dietl et al., "The Inner Workings of the Hydrazine Synthase Multiprotein Complex," *Nature* 527, no. 7578 (2015): 394, https://www.nature.com/articles/nature15517.

3. Laura van Niftrik and Mike S. M. Jetten, "Anaerobic Ammonium-Oxidizing Bacteria: Unique Microorganisms with Exceptional Properties," *Microbiology Molecular Biology Reviews* 76, no. 3 (2012): 586, https://mmbr.asm.org/content/76/3/585.

4. Mike S. M. Jetten et al., "Biochemistry and Molecular Biology of Anammox Bacteria," *Critical Reviews in Biochemistry and Molecular Biology*, 44, no. 2–3 (June 2009), 65.

5. Jetten et al., "Biochemistry and Molecular Biology of Anammox," 65–84.

6. Marcel M. M. Kuypers et al., "Anaerobic Ammonium Oxidation by Anammox Bacteria in the Black Sea," *Nature* 422 (2003): 608–611. See also Laura van Niftrik and Mike S. M. Jetten, "Anaerobic Ammonium-Oxidizing Bacteria: Unique Microorganisms with Exceptional Properties," *Microbiology Molecular Biology Reviews* 76, no. 3 (2012): 585–596.

7. Van Niftrik and Jetten, "Anaerobic Ammonium-Oxidizing Bacteria," 585.

8. For more on hydrazine properties and uses see "Hydrazine," *PubChem Compound Database*, National Center for Biotechnology Information, accessed Sept. 20, 2018, https://pubchem.ncbi.nlm.nih.gov/compound/hydrazine#section=Top.

9. Laura A. van Niftrik et al., "The Anammoxosome: An Intracytoplasmic Compartment in Anammox Bacteria," *FEMS Microbiology Letters* 233, no. 1 (2004): 7–13.

10. Jaap S. Sinninghe Damsté et al., "Linearly Concatenated Cyclobutane Lipids Form a Dense Bacterial Membrane," *Nature* 419 (2002): 708–712.

11. Jack van de Vossenberg et al., "Enrichment and Characterization of Marine Anammox Bacteria Associated with Global Nitrogen Gas Production," *Environmental Microbiology* 10, no. 11 (2008): 3120.

12. "Rocket Science in a Microbe Saves the Planet," *Evolution News & Science Today*, November 23, 2015, https://evolutionnews.org/2015/11/rocket_science_1/; "Tagish Lake

Meteorite Does Not Solve Homochirality Problem," *Evolution News & Science Today*, July 30, 2012, https://evolutionnews.org/2015/11/rocket_science_1/t.

13. Andreas Dietl et al., "The Inner Workings of the Hydrazine Synthase Multiprotein Complex," *Nature* 527 (November 2015), 394.

14. "Rocket Science in a Microbe."

15. Holger Daims et al., "Complete Nitrification by Nitrospira Bacteria," *Nature* 528 (2015): 504–509.

16. Joseph Stromberg, "This Insect Has the Only Mechanical Gears Ever Found in Nature," *Smithsonian Magazine*, September 12, 2013, https://www.smithsonianmag.com/science-nature/this-insect-has-the-only-mechanical-gears-ever-found-in-nature-6480908/#Jh26s1gRI4ObrI15.99.

17. Malcolm Burrows and Gregory Sutton, "Interacting Gears Synchronize Propulsive Leg Movements in a Jumping Insect," *Science*, 341, no. 6151 (September 2013), 1254.

18. University of Cambridge, "Functioning 'Mechanical Gears' Seen in Nature for the First Time," September 12, 2013, https://www.cam.ac.uk/research/news/functioning-mechanical-gears-seen-in-nature-for-the-first-time.

19. Jo Marchant, "Decoding the Antikythera Mechanism, the First Computer," *Smithsonian Magazine*, February 2015, https://www.smithsonianmag.com/history/decoding-antikythera-mechanism-first-computer-180953979/.

20. "Tyson Shrimp on TV," July 2, 1999, *Great Yarmouth News*, Town Centre Partnership, http://gytcp.co.uk/news/tyson-shrimp-on-tv-710.html.

21. S. N. Patek, W. L. Korff, and R. L. Caldwell, "Biomechanics: Deadly Strike Mechanism of a Mantis Shrimp," *Nature* 428 (2004): 819–820.

22. Ella Davies, "The Most Powerful Punches and Kicks of All Time," *Earth*, BBC, June 6, 2017, http://www.bbc.com/earth/story/20170605-the-most-powerful-punches-and-kicks-of-all-time.

23. Ed Yong, "How Mantis Shrimps Deliver Armour-Shattering Punches without Breaking Their Fists," *Discover*, June 7, 2012, http://blogs.discovermagazine.com/notrocketscience/2012/06/07/how-mantis-shrimps-deliver-armour-shattering-punches-without-breaking-their-fists/#.W9IHrGhKhPY.

24. T. I. Zack, T. Claverie, S. N. Patek, "Elastic Energy Storage in the Mantis Shrimp's Fast Predatory Strike," *Journal of Experimental Biology* 212 (2009): 4002–4009.

25. Ella Davies, "The Most Powerful Punches."

26. Ed Yong, "The Mantis Shrimp Has the World's Fastest Punch," *National Geographic*, June 19, 2008, https://www.nationalgeographic.com/science/phenomena/2008/07/19/the-mantis-shrimp-has-the-worlds-fastest-punch/?user.testname=lazyloading:1.

27. Zack, "Elastic Energy Storage in the Mantis Shrimp's Fast Predatory Strike."

28. Yong, "The Mantis Shrimp Has the World's Fastest Punch."

29. James C. Weaver et al., "The Stomatopod Dactyl Club: A Formidable Damage-Tolerant Biological Hammer," *Science* 336, no. 6086 (2012): 1275–80.

30. Yong, "How Mantis Shrimps Deliver Armour-Shattering Punches."

31. Ed Yong, "The Mantis Shrimp Has the World's Fastest Punch."

32. John Brittnacher, "What are Carnivorous Plants?" International Carnivorous Plant Society, January 2010, http://www.carnivorousplants.org/cp/carnivory/what. For an encyclopedic work that covers the ecology, diversity, and natural history of carnivorous plants

see Stewart McPherson, *Carnivorous Plants and Their Habitats*, vols. 1 and 2, eds. Andreas Fleischmann and Alastair Robinson (Dorset, UK: Redfern Natural History Productions Ltd., 2010).

33. Aaron M. Ellison and Nicholas J. Gotelli, "Energetics and the Evolution of Carnivorous Plants—Darwin's 'Most Wonderful Plants in the World,'" *Journal of Experimental Botany* 60, no. 1 (2009): 21.

34. Brittnacher, "What are Carnivorous Plants?"

35. For a detailed description of this plant see "*Dionaea muscipula*—The Venus Flytrap," *Botanical Society of America*, https://botany.org/Carnivorous_Plants/venus_flytrap.php.

36. R. Hedrich and E. Neher, "Venus Flytrap: How an Excitable, Carnivorous Plant Works," *Trends in Plant Science*, 23, no 3 (2018): 220.

37. The Figure 5.4 cycle scheme was adapted from Hedrich and Erwin, "Venus Flytrap," 220–234.

38. Aaron M. Ellison and Nicholas J. Gotelli, "Energetics and the Evolution of Carnivorous Plants—Darwin's 'Most Wonderful Plants in the World,'" *Journal of Experimental Botany* 60, no. 1 (2009): 19.

39. Brittnacher, "What are Carnivorous Plants?"

40. For more examples of devolution, and the problem this pattern poses for modern evolutionary theory, see Michel Behe, *Darwin Devolves: The New Science about DNA That Challenges Evolution* (San Francisco: HarperOne, 2019).

6. Birds: A Case Study in Foresight

1. Anders Hedenström et al., "Annual 10-Month Aerial Life Phase in the Common Swift *Apus apus*," *Current Biology* 26, no. 22 (2016): 3066–3070.

2. Wolfgang Wiltschko and Roswitha Wiltschko, "Magnetic Orientation in Birds," *Journal of Experimental Biology* 199, pt. 1 (1996): 29–38.

3. Anja Günther et al., "Double-Cone Localization and Seasonal Expression Pattern Suggest a Role in Magnetoreception for European Robin Cryptochrome 4," *Current Biology* 28 (2018): 211–223; Atticus Pinzon-Rodriguez, Staffan Bensch, and Rachel Muheim, "Expression Patterns of Cryptochrome Genes in Avian Retina Suggest Involvement of Cry4 in Light-dependent Magnetoreception," *Journal of The Royal Society Interface* 15, no. 140 (2018): 20180058.

4. David Kaiser, "Is Quantum Entanglement Real?" *New York Times*, Nov. 14, 2014, https://www.nytimes.com/2014/11/16/opinion/sunday/is-quantum-entanglement-real.html.

5. Albert Einstein, Boris Podolsky, and Nathan Rosen, "Can Quantum-Mechanical Description of Physical Reality be Considered Complete?" *Physical Review* 47 (1935): 777.

6. Juan Yin et al., "Lower Bound on the Speed of Nonlocal Correlations without Locality and Measurement Choice Loopholes," *Physical Review Letters* 110 (2013): 260407.

7. Klaus Schulten and Albert Weller, "Exploring Fast Electron Transfer Processes by Magnetic Fields," *Biophysical Journal* 24 (1978): 295–305.

8. Brian Brocklehurst and Keith Alan McLauchlan, "Free Radical Mechanism for the Effects of Environmental Electromagnetic Fields on Biological Systems," *International Journal of Radiation Biology* 69 (1996): 3–24.

9. Thorsten Ritz, Salih Adem, and Klaus Schulten, "A Model for Photoreceptor-Based Magnetoreception in Birds," *Biophysical Journal* 78 (2000): 707–718.

10. Erik M. Gauger et al., "Sustained Quantum Coherence Entanglement in the Avian Compass," *Physical Review Letters* 106 (2011): 040503.

11. Lisa Grossman, "In the Blink of Bird's Eye, A Model for Quantum Navigation," *Wired*, January 27, 2011, https://www.wired.com/2011/01/quantum-birds/.

12. Fred Hoyle, "The Universe: Past and Present Reflections," *Annual Review of Astronomy and Astrophysics* 20 (1982): 16.

13. P. Hunton, "Research on Eggshell Structure and Quality: An Historical Overview," *Revista Brasileira de Ciencias Avicolas* 7, no. 2 (2005): 67.

14. "How Birds Get Oxygen Inside Their Eggs," NPR's Skunk Bear, April 17, 2018, https://youtu.be/w-M33PtwtM4.

15. Gail Damerow, "What is an Egg Tooth?" *Cackle Hatchery*, August 26, 2016, https://blog.cacklehatchery.com/what-is-an-egg-tooth/.

16. Damerow, "What is an Egg Tooth?"

17. Damerow, "What is an Egg Tooth?"

18. Damerow, "What is an Egg Tooth?" Once the chick has broken free of the shell, its beak will continue to strengthen and grow. However, the egg tooth stops growing after hatching, drying up and falling off a few days later.

19. Quoted in Tim Birkhead, *The Most Perfect Thing: Inside (and Outside) a Bird's Egg* (New York: Bloomsbury, 2016), preface.

20. For some highly speculative scenarios on egg evolution, see: Mary C. Stoddard et al., "Avian Egg Shape: Form, Function, and Evolution," *Science* 356, no. 6344 (2017): 1249–54; David J. Varricchio and Frankie D. Jackson, "Reproduction in Mesozoic Birds and Evolution of the Modern Avian Reproductive Mode," *The Auk* 133, no. 4 (10 August 2016): 654–84.

7. FORESIGHT IN THE HUMAN FORM: REPRODUCTION

1. Jeffrey A. Riffell, Patrick J. Krug, and Richard K. Zimmer, "The Ecological and Evolutionary Consequences of Sperm Chemoattraction," *Proceedings of the National Academy of Science* 101, no. 13 (2004): 4501–6.

2. Janice P. Evans and Harvey M. Florman, "The State of the Union: The Cell Biology of Fertilization," *Nature Cell Biology & Nature Medicine* 8, S1 (2002): S57–S63.

3. Michael J. Seckl, Neil J. Sebire, and Ross S. Berkowitz, "Gestational Trophoblastic Disease," *The Lancet* 376, no. 9742 (2010): 717–29.

4. Sarah Knapton, "Fertility Breakthrough: Scientists Discover How Sperm and Egg Bind," *The Telegraph*, April 16, 2014, https://www.telegraph.co.uk/news/science/science-news/10771028/Fertility-breakthrough-scientists-discover-how-sperm-and-egg-bind.html.

5. "Your Guide to Pregnancy Hormones: What to Expect," *What to Expect*, September 15, 2016, https://www.whattoexpect.com/pregnancy/pregnancy-health/pregnancy-hormones.aspx.

6. Phyllis C. Leppert, "Anatomy and Physiology of Cervical Ripening," *Clinical Obstetrics and Gynecology* 38, no. 2 (1995): 267–79.

7. Pei-Yun Tsai et al., "IL-22 Upregulates Epithelial Claudin-2 to Drive Diarrhea and Enteric Pathogen Clearance," *Cell Host & Microbe* 21, no. 6 (2017): 671–81.

8. Haruka Ishimoto et al., "Claudin-2 Expression Is Upregulated in the Ileum of Diarrhea Predominant Irritable Bowel Syndrome Patients," *Journal of Clinical Biochemistry and Nutrition* 60, no. 2 (2017): 146–50.

9. Charles Darwin, *The Descent of Man*, 1st ed. (London: John Murray, 1871), 27.

10. A recent global survey has suggested that appendicitis has been much less common in developing countries and that "the epidemiologic patterns of appendicitis support the notion that appendicitis is driven by multifactorial environmental triggers associated with the industrialization of society." See Mollie Ferris et al., "The Global Incidence of Appendicitis: A Systematic Review of Population-Based Studies," *Annals of Surgery* 266, no. 2 (2017): 241.

11. Johan Styrud et al., "Appendectomy versus Antibiotic Treatment in Acute Appendicitis: A Prospective Multicenter Randomized Controlled Trial," *World Journal of Surgery* 30, no. 6 (2006): 1033–37.

12. Nicholas B. Hanson and Dennis K. Lanning, "Microbial Induction of B and T Cell Areas in Rabbit Appendix," *Developmental & Comparative Immunology* 32, no. 8 (2008): 980–91.

13. Heather F. Smith et al., "Morphological Evolution of the Mammalian Cecum and Cecal Appendix," *Comptes Rendus Palevol* 16, no. 1 (2017): 39–57; R. Randal Bolliger et al., "Biofilms in the Large Bowel Suggest an Apparent Function of the Human Vermiform Appendix," *Journal of Theoretical Biology* 249, no. 4 (2007): 826–31.

14. Gregory P. Donaldson, S. Melanie Lee, and Sarkis K. Mazmanian, "Gut Biogeography of the Bacterial Microbiota," *Nature Reviews Microbiology* 14, no. 1 (2016): 20–32.

8. Planning for the Senses

1. Jennifer Leong, "Number of Colors Distinguishable by the Human Eye," The Physics Factbook, 2006, https://hypertextbook.com/facts/2006/JenniferLeong.shtml.

2. Leong, "Number of Colors."

3. Gunter Wyszecki, *Color* (Chicago: World Book Inc., 2006), 824.

4. Aristotle, *On the Soul*, trans. J. A. Smith, book 2, The Internet Classics Archive, http://classics.mit.edu//Aristotle/soul.html.

5. Charles Darwin, *The Descent of Man, and Selection in Relation to Sex* (London: John Murray, 1871), 17.

6. Gordon M. Shepherd, "The Human Sense of Smell: Are We Better Than We Think?" *PLoS Biology* 2 (2004): e146.

7. John P. McGann, "Poor Human Olfaction Is a 19th-Century Myth," *Science* 356, no. 6338 (2017): eaam7263.

8. McGann, "Poor Human Olfaction."

9. Trina J. Lapis, Michael H. Penner, and Juyun Lim, "Humans Can Taste Glucose Oligomers Independent of the hT1R2/hT1R3 Sweet Taste Receptor," *Chemical Senses* 41(9) (2016): 755–762.

10. P. Dalton et al., "The Merging of the Senses: Integration of Subthreshold Taste and Smell," *Nature Neuroscience* 3 (2000): 431–32.

11. Jürgen Krieger and Heinz Breer, "Olfactory Reception in Invertebrates," *Science* 286, no. 5440 (1999): 720–23.

12. Karl P. N. Shuker, *The Hidden Powers of Animals: Uncovering the Secrets of Nature* (London: Marshall, 2001).

13. Monika Stengl, "Pheromone Transduction in Moths," *Frontiers in Cellular Neuroscience* 4 (2010): 133.

14. Stengl, "Pheromone Transduction in Moths," 133.

15. Steven Linton, *Understanding Pain for Better Clinical Practice: A Psychological Perspective* (New York: Elsevier Health Sciences, 2005).

16. Jennifer L. Hellier, ed., *The Five Senses and Beyond: The Encyclopedia of Perception* (Santa Barbara: Greenwood, 2016).

17. Steven Pete, "Congenital Analgesia: The Agony of Feeling No Pain," *BBC News*, July 17, 2012, http://www.bbc.com/news/magazine-18713585; Rogene Fisher, "Does Pain Serve a Purpose?" *ABC News*, May 13, 2005, http://abcnews.go.com/Health/PainManagement/story?id=741257&page=1.

18. Ya-Chun Chen et al., "Transcriptional Regulator PRDM12 is Essential for Human Pain Perception," *Nature Genetics* 47 (2015): 803–8.

19. Mo Costandi, "Uncomfortably Numb: The People Who Feel No Pain," *The Guardian*, May 25, 2015, https://www.theguardian.com/science/neurophilosophy/2015/may/25/the-people-who-feel-no-pain. See also Mazen Kurban et al., "A Nonsense Mutation in the *SCN9A* Gene in Congenital Insensitivity to Pain," *Dermatology* 221 (2010): 179–83.

20. Mehran Karimi and Razieh Fa Llah, "A Case Report of Congenital Insensitivity to Pain and Anhidrosis (CIPA)," *Iranian Journal of Child Neurology* 6, no. 43 (2012): 45.

21. Karimi and Llah, "A Case Report," 45–48; Mukund D. Rahalkar, Anand M. Rahalkar, and S. K. Joshi, "Case Series: Congenital Insensitivity to Pain and Anhidrosis," *Indian Journal of Radiology and Imaging* 18, no. 2 (2008): 132–34; Leema R. Peddareddygari, Kinsi Oberoi, and Raji P. Grewal, "Congenital Insensitivity to Pain: A Case Report and Review of the Literature Case," *Reports in Neurological Medicine* 141953 (2014).

22. See Sarah Novotny and Len Kravitz, "The Science of Breathing," available on Kravitz's University of New Mexico page https://www.unm.edu/~lkravitz/Article%20folder/Breathing.html; see also Neil S. Cherniack et al., "The Mechanics of Breathing," *Encyclopaedia Britannica*, https://www.britannica.com/science/human-respiratory-system/The-mechanics-of-breathing; "IAQUK Resources – Respiratory System," IAQUK, http://www.iaquk.org.uk/ResourcesRespiratory.html.

23. "IAQUK Resources – Respiratory System."

24. Novotny and Kravitz, "The Science of Breathing."

25. Novotny and Kravitz, "The Science of Breathing"; Jorge Gallego, Elise Nsegbe, and Estelle Durand, "Learning in Respiratory Control," *Behavior Modification* 25, no. 4 (2001): 495–512.

26. Adam E. Ziemann et al., "The Amygdala Is a Chemosensor that Detects Carbon Dioxide and Acidosis to Elicit Fear Behavior," *Cell* 139, no. 5 (2009): 1012–21, https://doi.org/10.1016/j.cell.2009.10.029.

27. Cell Press, "Brain's Fear Center is Equipped with Built-in Suffocation Sensor," *ScienceDaily*, November 26, 2009, http://www.sciencedaily.com/releases/2009/11/091125134651.htm.

28. Jordan W. Smoller et al., "The Human Ortholog of Acid-Sensing Ion Channel Gene ASIC1a Is Associated with Panic Disorder and Amygdala Structure and Function," *Biological Psychiatry* 76, no. 11 (2014), 902–10.

29. Cell Press, "Brain's Fear Center."

9. Foresight and the Future of Science

1. Vladimir Matveev, "Development of a Chicken Embryo," YouTube video, 2:06, May 25, 2008, https://www.youtube.com/watch?v=LKvez9duEHQ; Yusaku Watanabe, "Observation of the Development of Chick Embryo," YouTube video, 9:45, November 26, 2017, https://www.youtube.com/watch?v=uE0uKvUbcfw.

2. Stephen C. Meyer, *Darwin's Doubt: The Explosive Origin of Animal Life and the Case for Intelligent Design* (San Francisco: HarperOne, 2013), 328–9.

3. Michael Behe, *Darwin Devolves: The New Science about DNA That Challenges Evolution* (San Francisco: HarperOne, 2019).

4. For more on the problems facing the various post-Neo-Darwinian models, and why most of them are not really post-Neo-Darwinian models, see chapters 4 and 5 of Behe, *Darwin Devolves*, 93–137, and chapters 15 and 16 of Meyer, *Darwin's Doubt*, 291–335.

5. *Cosmos*, "The Shores of the Cosmic Ocean," 1. Directed by David Oyster et al. Written by Carl Sagan, Ann Druyan, and Steven Soter. PBS, September 28, 1980.

6. Francisco Ayala, "Chance and Necessity," *Counterbalance*, http://www.counterbalance.org/evolution/chance-frame.html.

7. J. J. Thomson, "Inaugural Address," The British Association at Winnipeg, *Nature* 81 (August 26, 1909), 257.

ACKNOWLEDGMENTS

I AM DEEPLY THANKFUL TO SO MANY WHO CONTRIBUTED TO THIS book. In Brazil, I must acknowledge Enézio Almeida Filho for launching ID in the country and Augustus Nicodemus Lopes for organizing at Mackenzie University the first ever Brazilian ID conferences. For catalyzing the book by creating in 2017 the Discovery-Mackenzie Center for Research on Science, Faith and Society, and for inviting me to be its coordinator, I am also very grateful to Davi Charles Gomes (chancellor) and Benedito Guimarães Aguiar Neto (head of Mackenzie University).

At Discovery Institute USA I am eternally grateful to Jonathan Witt for his advice, wonderful contributions as to style, reorganization of chapters and figures, and selection of arguments. Thanks as well to Rachel Adams, who did the initial pass through the manuscript, helping with reorganization and trimming, correcting my poor English, and getting the prose closer to lucid and polished English (a big job indeed). I also am deeply thankful to scientists Jonathan Wells, Ann Gauger, Guillermo Gonzalez, Ray Bohlin, Scott Minnich, Matti Leisola, Michael Behe, and Brian Miller, as well as physician Howard Glicksman, for providing advice on particular sections. Thanks as well to a superb proofreader. (I've kept his name out due to risks of academic persecution.)

I cannot neglect to mention Michael Behe, Stephen Meyer, Jonathan Wells, William Dembski, Michael Denton, and Douglas Axe for inspiring ID books, Mike Perry for the great layout, Brian Gage for the charming cover art, Otniel Araújo for the great illustrations, and John West, the Associate Director of Discovery Institute's Center for Science and Culture, for all his support and for inviting me to write this book based on a talk I gave at the 2017 Alberta ID meeting.

ILLUSTRATION CREDITS

All illustrations by Otniel Araújo, except for Figure 2.2 and
    Figure 6.1.
Figure 2.2: Adobe Stock/gallinago_media.
Figure 6.1: Adobe Stock/Creative Mood.

INDEX

A

Abegg, Adam, 140
Abrão, Maurício Simões, 6
Acrosome, 111–112
Activation energy, 67
Adem, Salih, 102
Aizawa, Shin-Ichi, 81
Amino acids, 65–66
Amino esters, 59–61
Anammox bacteria, 84–86
Anammoxosomes, 85–86
Antikythera mechanism, 91
Appendix, human, 119–121, 138
Apus apus, 99
Aquaporins, 21–24
Aristotle, 125
ASIC1a, 134
Atmosphere, 33–35
Augusti, Rodinei, 5
Autotrophs, 84
Avian compass, 102
Ayala, Francisco, 145

B

Bacterial flagellum motor, 77–83
Baker, David, 70
Ball, Philip, 53
Behe, Michael, 77, 80, 141
Bemer, Robert, 62

Benjamin, Simon, 102
Bird
  egg, 103–107
  navigation, 99–103
Boyle, Robert, 146
Brazilian Mass Spectrometry
  Society, 13
Brittnacher, John, 95
Broca, Paul, 125
Brocklehurst, Brian, 102
Buckminsterfullerene, 102
Buckyball, 102
Burrows, Malcolm, 88–89

C

Carbon cycle, 83
Carnivorous plants, 94–98
Carnivory, 96–97
Cellular DNA, 45–47
Cervical dilation, 117–119
Chance and necessity, 145
Chaperones and chaperonins,
  70–74, 138
Chick embryo, 137–138
Chicken or egg, 107–108, 137
Claudin-2 protein, 120
Claverie, T., 92
Cnidarians, 130
Comammox bacteria, 87

Cooption model, 80
Copernicus, Nicolaus, 146
Corpus luteum, 115–116
Costandi, Mo, 130
Crick, Francis, 62
Cry4, 100–102
Cryptochromes, 100–102
Cytosine degradation, 54–56

D

Damerow, Gail, 106
Darlingtonia, 97
Darwin, Charles, 50, 68, 95, 119, 120, 125
Darwin Devolves, 141
Darwin's Black Box, 80
Deoxyribose for DNA, 51–52
Descent of Man, The, 120
Diarrhea, 119–121, 138
Dietl, Andreas, 86
DNA, 138
  cellular, 45–47
  efficiency of, 61–62
  four bases, 51–52
  to RNA, 69

E

E. coli, 77
Egg
  breathing, 103–105
  tooth, 105–107
Einstein, Albert, 101
Ellison, Aaron, 95, 97
Ellis, R. J., 76
Enzymes
  conjugated, 68

DNA, 48
  need for, 67–70
Epigenetic inheritance, 139
Ertl, Gerhard, 6
Estrogen, 116
Evolutionary developmental biology (evo-devo), 139
Eyes, human, 123–124

F

Feringa, Bernard L., 59
Fine tuning, 26–28
Flagellar filament caps, 77–83
Flagellum, 80
Flew, Antony, 62
Follicle-stimulating hormone (FSH), 115
Foresight and intelligence, 142
Foresight-or-Death Principle, 141–142
Fuller, Buckminster, 102
Fullerene, 102

G

Galileo Galilei, 146
Gastrointestinal (GI) tract, 120–121
Gauger, Ann, 7
Gears in insects, 87–91, 138
Genetic redundancy, 56–59
Glycoproteins, 111
Gotelli, Nicholas, 95, 97
GroES and GroEL, 74
Gurdon, John B., 5

H

Hammarström, Per, 74

Hartl, F. Ulrich, 75

Heat shock protein (HSP), 73

Hedrich, Rainer, 95

Heterotrophs, 84

Higginson, Thomas Wentworth, 107

Homochirality, 53–54, 66–67

Homoplasy, 95

Homoviscous adaptation, 16

Hoyle, Fred, 27, 103

HSP70, 72, 75

Human chorionic gonadotropin hormone (hCG), 116

Human placental lactogen (hPL), 116

Hydrazine, 85, 138

I

Insectivorous Plants, 95

Intelligent design, 143

Interleukin-22 protein, 120

International Carnivorous Plant Society, 97

International Mass Spectrometry Foundation, 13

Issus, 88–91

Izumo protein, 113–114

J

Jetten, Mike, 84–87

Josephson, Brian David, 5

Juno protein, 113–114

K

Kaiser, David, 101

Kepler, Johannes, 146

Kisalius, David, 93

L

lac operon, 63–65

Ladderanes, 86

Leong, Jennifer, 124

Lewis and Clark expedition, 131

Lightning, 39–45

Lindahl, Tomas, 58

Luteinizing hormone (LH), 115

Lynch, Michael, 140

M

Magnetoreception, 99

Maki-Yonekura, Saori, 79

Mansy, Sheref, 15, 20

Mantis shrimp, 91–95, 138

Martins, Daniela de Luna, 7

McGann, John, 125–126

McLauchlan, Keith Alan, 102

Megapode bird, 106

Mendoza, Diego de, 16

Meyer, Stephen, 140

Microbe paradox, 83–84

Miller, Kenneth, 80–81

Modrich, Paul, 58

Moran, Laurence, 72, 73, 75–77

Morse code, 62

Morse, Samuel F. B., 62

Mota, Kelson, 7

Moth, sense of smell, 126

Mount Improbable, 23

Mulkidjanian, A. Y., 21
Multiverse, 42–44, 144–145

N
Namba, Keiichi, 79
Nanomachine, 59
Natural genetic engineering, 139
Neher, Erwin, 95
Neo-Darwinism, 139
Nepenthes, 97
Neto, Brenno A. D., 6
Neutral evolution (non-adaptive evolution), 139–141
Newton, Isaac, 146
Niftrik, Laura van, 84–87
Nitrogen cycle, 83–84, 86
Nociceptors, 130–131
Nymphalid planthopper, 88

O
Odontodactylus scyllarus, 91
Onken, Michael, 54
Operon, 63–65
Oxygen, 131–135
Oxygen shield for cells, 14–18
Oxytocin, 117
Ozone, 35–39

P
Pain, 128–131
Patek, Sheila, 92
Pauli Exclusion Principle, 30
Pentacycloanammoxic acid, 86
Phosphate anion, 47–49
Phospholipids, 17–21

Podolsky, Boris, 101
Pregnancy hormones, 114–117
Progesterone, 116
Prolactin, 117
Prostaglandins, 118
Punctuated equilibrium, 139

Q
Quantum mechanics, 101, 138
Quinlan, R. A., 76

R
Racemic mixture, 53, 65–66
Raschig process, 86
Relaxin, 116
Reproduction, human, 109–119, 138
Ribose, 49–50
Ribose for RNA, 51–52
Ribosome, 59–61
Ritz, Thorsten, 102
RNA World, 55
Rosen, Nathan, 101

S
Sagan, Carl, 144
Sancar, Aziz, 58
Sand, George, 33
Sauvage, Jean-Pierre, 59
Schulten, Klaus, 102
SCN9A gene, 130
Self-organization (evolutionary), 139
Shapiro, James, 65
Smell and taste, 124–126

Stengl, Monika, 127–128
Stoddart, J. Fraser, 59
Sutton, Gregory, 88–89
Swift (bird), 99

T
Thomson, J. J., 146
Trigger Factor, 72

V
Venus flytrap, 95–96

W
Water, 28–33
  floating ice, 32–34
  super-solvent, 30–31
Wemmie, John, 134
Woodland, Norman Joseph, 62

Y
Yonekura, Koji, 79
Yong, Ed, 92–114

Z
Zack, T. I., 92
Zona pellucida, 111

Made in the USA
Coppell, TX
05 March 2021